REINCARNATION
The Journey to Perfection

by Chris Meyer

Cover Quote:
The Katha Upanishad 1.1.20

First Edition Revised

Copyright 2020

Henson Creek
Publishing

Table of Contents

Preface	i
Introduction	1
Contemplating Life's Mysteries	7
Reincarnation: The Beginning	15
Reincarnation: A Basic Understanding	25
Reincarnation and the Laws of the Universe	35
God and the Soul	43
Does God Exist?	47
Does the Soul Exist?	69
Reincarnation and God	83
The Concept of One Life	89
The Concept of One Reality	93
Why We Aren't Perfect	94
Reincarnation and Physical Existence	99
Reincarnation and the Afterlife	105
Reincarnation and Heredity	115
The Parent/Child Relationship	118
Reincarnation and Inequality	123
Reincarnation and Justice	129
Who Judges?	138
Pain and Suffering in Children	141
Reincarnation and Time	145
Reincarnation and Perfection	151
The Wealthy and Perfection	156
Finding Peace in Life	156
Reincarnation and Predestination	158
Reincarnation: The Conclusion	165

Preface

I begin this discourse fully realizing the challenges that I face in my effort to present to the Western world a philosophy that is so alien to those who are already intimately familiar with other, more popular ideologies. But since I am compelled to do so, I will endeavor to be clear and concise in sharing what I know, what I have discovered and what has been revealed to me concerning this remarkable doctrine.

I fully understand that the mere mention of the word "Reincarnation" conjures up mystical and bizarre images, as well as tales of ancient rituals and mysterious ceremonies, and men reborn as animals or other creatures. It is one of the most misunderstood ancient philosophies, especially in the Western world where it has received very little attention, or has been confronted with hostility by those religions or ideologies that are more widely accepted. However, as I will explain, it is the most reasonable and logical life/death philosophy that exists today.

But first, I should like to explain why I have taken the time to write this book. I am a skeptic. It's not that I enjoy being a skeptic. I simply find that I cannot accept things on face value. I refuse to be misled, whether intentionally or unintentionally. I refuse to be part of the herd no matter how comfortable it is to be one. If I am going to believe in something, especially something that will significantly impact my life—the way I think or act, then it must be sufficiently substantiated by legitimate sources. It must provide more than emotional bliss, ceremonial drama or the endorsement of tradition.

I have not always been a skeptic, but somewhere in my religious journey, I became one. It actually occurred in the later years of my life. As a matter of fact, I was fervently religious throughout my youth and much of my early adult life, taking on a role of responsibility and leadership in the Protestant faith that I had chosen, or, I should say, was hereditarily chosen for me. However, in the course of my studies, I became increasingly aware that there were inconsistencies in the doctrine of my faith that I could no longer justify. And so, I began a journey to find a religion that offered me something that satisfied the skeptic that I had become. A religion that provided the truth, if such a religion actually existed. A religion that offered reason over emotionalism, although I did so much enjoy the emotional ecstasy that revelational religion provides.

As a result, I spent the next few decades of my life studying various religions, both ancient as well as contemporary, in search of one ideology that would provide real answers to life's crucial questions. I have searched for God through the eyes of reason and logic. I have sought a doctrine that is believable and reasonable; a creed that complies with reality as we experience it; that makes sense; that doesn't demand that we set aside our intelligence; and that treats the concept of God as something other than an entity that behaves more like a human than a god. In short, a religion or philosophy that provides truth; because if an ideology deals with life and death it must be credible, unlocking the mysteries of life and providing us with realistic guidance now and in the future.

Unfortunately, I did not find a religion that met my expectations. Everything I encountered seemed to me to be filled with fairytales and unrealistic promises. So I turned to philosophy, the science of life. There, I stumbled across a doctrine that caught my attention; one that seemed at first glance to offer credible answers to many of life's deepest questions, while at the same time, provided the kind of hope that is such a valuable benefit of religion; a philosophy that made the perils of life and the inevitability of death coalesce in such a way that they make sense. Reincarnation is that philosophy.

And so, I now feel obligated to share that philosophy with those who might be traveling on the same journey as I; not with the goal of evangelizing or winning converts, but for the sole purpose of sharing what I believe is the most reasonable philosophy that exists concerning life and death; a doctrine that is not of men, but rather whose principles have been written by the Creator and substantiated by the laws of the universe. While this is a most ancient doctrine, I feel that it is a duty to offer it once again in a simple and concise manner to our modern world.

I would also like to begin this discourse with a clarification. We must all realize that everything we hear; everything that is taught or asserted by any priest, or preacher, or Imam, or sage, or philosopher concerning what happens to the Soul following physical death is nothing more than speculation. Even those who claim to have had a "near death" experience must be addressed with caution, acknowledging that what they actually experienced might have been nothing more than an unconscious episode where the brain lapsed into a deep sleep and the visions that were recalled after awakening were anything more than images of what they desired the afterlife to be, or were reflections of things that had been planted in their memory at a previous time and then repressed in the subconscious only to be recalled when awakened, but nothing more than a dream.

All theories of what happens to us after this life, if anything, are speculation. Likewise, just as those who offer a theory for what lies beyond are speculating, those who believe that there is *nothing* beyond this earthly life are also speculating. So what exists beyond this life, if anything, is uncertain. I offer this preface so all those who read this discourse will understand that what is offered in the following pages should also be viewed as speculation.

However, having said that, it is also true that some speculations are more credible than others. In other words, the more objective[1] evidence there is to support an assumption, the more credible that assumption becomes. It is unreasonable to accept any philosophy or theory that has no supporting objective evidence, even if—and especially if it concerns metaphysical concepts.

Even though I do touch briefly on how Reincarnation addresses what might occur in the afterlife, I concentrate my discussion on how this concept affects physical life and non-physical existence now and in the future; and how the experience of life and death blend together to provide both with a well-defined purpose; because as we can see from the efficient functioning of the universe, everything has a purpose[2], a reason for being. So, it should also be with life and death.

---

[1] I use the term "Objective" to mean not influenced by personal feelings or opinions in considering and representing facts.
[2] Everything has a purpose in a particular time and place. That purpose might change through the course of God's evolutionary plan. Parts of a whole might be modified or become purposeless, but the whole of the parts will evolve to perform or serve a specific purpose.

While there are many who are not ready to hear or capable of understanding this philosophy, and while there are still others who will find this doctrine in conflict with other ideologies, I am certain that there are many who are ready to be exposed to this amazing doctrine—a philosophy of truth that solves some of the greatest mysteries of life. I ask only that you read this thesis with an open mind, acknowledging that any philosophy we choose to believe should make sense and be reasonable; one that elevates us to a higher level of existence.

In his book, *A Study in Human Evolution: The Resurrection of the Body and The Reincarnation of the Soul*, Dr. Théophile Pascal writes:

> "To every awakened soul the question comes: Why does evil exist? So long as the enigma remains unsolved, suffering remains a threatening sphinx, opposing God and ready to devour mankind. The key to the secret lies in Evolution, which can be accomplished only by means of the continual return of souls to earth. When once man learns that suffering is the necessary result of divine manifestation; that inequalities of conditions are due to the different stages which beings have reached and the changeable action of their will; that the painful phase lasts only a moment in Eternity, and that we have it in our power to hasten its disappearance; that though slaves of the past, we are masters of the future; that, finally, the same glorious goal awaits all beings—then, despair will be at an end; hatred, envy, and rebellion

will have fled away, and peace will reign over a humanity made wise by knowledge."[3]

---

[3] Théophile Pascal. *Reincarnation: A Study in Human Evolution.*

"As a man, casting off worn out garments taketh new ones, so the dweller in the body, entereth into ones that are new."

— *Epictetus*

Introduction

The ultimate goal of life is happiness. Whether we acknowledge it consciously or not, happiness is the aspiration of every man and woman on the planet earth. Consequently, everything we do is an effort to bring us closer to that sensation of happiness, satisfaction, contentment. One key consideration in achieving that objective is selecting a philosophy or ideology that will serve to guide us through life; that will set our moral and ethical compass; that will inspire us and direct us when making important decisions; and that will shepherd us through the turbulent and perilous waters that will inevitably come as we journey through life. For this reason, the ideology that we choose must be trustworthy. We must have confidence that it is reliable and dependable to lead us in the right direction every time and in every situation. One that is consistent, reasonable and makes sense given what we know about the world in which we live.

Sadly, most people do not choose for themselves the creed or religion that will impact their life. For many, it is a matter of tradition, accepting what their family has always believed, or adhering to the religion that is the most prevalent in the geographic area where they live. For others, their commitment is a matter of emotion—a sensation or euphoria that inspires a sudden happiness. In his book, *The Varieties of Religious Experience: A Study in Human Nature*, psychologist William James gives this explanation for how a person might choose a particular belief:

> "When we think certain states of mind superior to others, is it ever because of what we know

> concerning their organic antecedents? No! it is always for two entirely different reasons. It is either because we take an immediate delight in them; or else it is because we believe them to bring us good consequential fruits for life."

In other words, the most important criteria are whether a belief makes us happy and fulfills a need in our life. Mystical euphoria and overwhelming emotionalism are among the religious sentiments that serve as determinates for many individuals when they select a creed. Unfortunately, initial impressions are not always dependable or representative of the total impact of a particular belief system. James stresses this point.

> "What immediately feels most "good" is not always most "true," when measured by the verdict of the rest of experience. The difference between Philip drunk and Philip sober is the classic instance in corroboration. If merely "feeling good" could decide, drunkenness would be the supremely valid human experience. But its revelations, however acutely satisfying at the moment, are inserted into an environment which refuses to bear them out for any length of time. The consequence of this discrepancy of the two criteria is the uncertainty which still prevails over so many of our spiritual judgments."

In other words, religions that inspire emotional highs have a tendency to also provide emotional lows—one moment feeling like one is in the very presence of God, while the next, when thrust into the turbulence of life, a feeling that God has disappeared altogether. The result can be depression and confusion. While extreme emotion enhances the religious experience, it should not be the only reason upon which such an important decision should be made.

Finally, there are those, and I believe that number has increased in recent times due to our current political and social environment, that are assessing or reassessing what they believe and why they believe it. Life has a way of forcing even the simplest mind to ponder the deeper questions of life, and it is at these times that one is inspired to search for a philosophy that reliably answers those questions in a practical and straightforward way.

That's the reason why I feel compelled to introduce this ancient philosophy with all of those who share the need for finding a believable and reasonable ideology; one that will bring happiness and peace, one that will endure the test of time and survive intense examination.

"The Hereafter never rises before the thoughtless child (the ignorant), deluded by the glamour of wealth. "This world alone is, there is none other": thinking thus, he falls under my sway again and again."

Death

Contemplating Life's Mysteries

What's the use? Life is meaningless. We work hard but seem to get nowhere. Relationships come and then suddenly disappear without warning. We watch as those who cheat, steal and lie become successful while those who are honorable and trustworthy are rewarded with failure and pity. We try to help others only to be taken advantage of. We make contributions to help the poor only to see them drift back into poverty. We feed the starving only to watch as they succumb to death, and so we realize that we have only prolonged life's agony and delayed the inevitable. We face hardships and trials that seem to have no positive resolution and so we find ourselves lost in depression—in a seemingly endless abyss with no hope of survival. We have no control. Why is one child born into poverty while another is born into wealth? Why is there such inequality in the world? Life isn't fair and justice isn't just. We look for hope in government, but soon realize that government is filled with liars. We turn to religion, but discover that religion is filled with unrealistic promises. And when all is done, rich or poor, intelligent or simple, we all eventually end up the same way: dust to dust, ashes to ashes. Death's appetite is never satisfied: young and old are subject to its indiscriminating grasp. Why are we here? What purpose do we serve? What accomplishments can we achieve that actually add value to life? And why must it all end in death? Questions such as these can destroy our happiness if they remain unanswered.

The deep philosophical questions of life have confounded mankind since the beginning of human consciousness. Where did we come from, why are we here, and where are we going are among those mysteries that have plagued the common and wise, the simple and the intelligent. And, over the thousands of years of philosophical arguments there have been a myriad of attempts to resolve these important questions. Unfortunately, the greatest number of these attempts have fallen short of providing answers that consistently and reasonably yield an understanding of how all of life's experiences, past and present, coalesce to render a logical explanation to life's mysteries. It is important for the answer to one of these questions to lead us to the answer of the others. In other words, knowing where we came from should also supply us with the reason for why we are here. And why we are here should help us understand where we are going. Additionally, such a philosophy that satisfactorily answers these basic questions should include the reasons for such things as why there is pain, why there is such unequal distribution of suffering and where can we find hope in a world where life appears to be so futile.

Throughout history, it has been science and religion that have attempted to answer these questions. Science endeavors to tell us *how* we came to be here but does little to explain *why* we came to be here. Perhaps, as some believe, there is no reason or purpose for human existence at all; we are a product of evolution by natural selection, exclusively, and we are here merely by chance. If this theory is true then there really is no reason for our existence. We are here by a throw of the dice and our lives are no more than a meaningless journey from birth to death. Our greatest contribution is the perpetuation of the species. In that case, we should eat, drink and be merry, or put another way, we should murder, rape and steal—get whatever we can and whatever we want. Why not? If life ends in death then why not attempt to live out every fantasy, pursue every selfish desire and allow emotion to dominate our decision-making and determine our short-lived destiny? After all, in death we all end up the same way: no rewards for good behavior and no consequences for bad.

For others, religion has attempted to provide guidance. For centuries it successfully pacified the masses offering an avenue of escape from earthly reality. Supported by governments and enforced by powerful church hierarchy, people cowered before God and church, submitting to the ideologies professed and promoted by the religion of their particular theocracy. With the goal of world evangelism and the promise of heaven to the faithful and hell to the unrighteous, parents indoctrinated their children and held firm to the faith of their forefathers. But religion failed to adapt to the changes of a rapidly evolving world where knowledge was abundant and intelligence was increasing. Without the support of government to endorse its authority and with the church losing its power to enforce compliance, the masses began to question doctrines that failed to comply with reality. Biblical stories began to sound more like fairytales than historical events. Inconsistencies in Koranic scriptures that spoke of Allah's love in one place but intolerance that condoned deadly violence in others were recognized by those possessing commonsense. Today, religions are seeing the greatest apostasy in the history of mankind[4]. The reason for this, especially among the

---

[4] Pew Research Center – Religious and Public Life. 2019

younger generation is that mainstream religions are not believable. They do not comply with reality as we know it. They simply do not make sense.

However, in spite of these shortcomings, religion remains a necessary part of life. Psychologist William James writes:

> "Religion thus makes easy and felicitous what in any case is necessary; and if it be the only agency that can accomplish this result, its vital importance as a human faculty stands vindicated beyond dispute. It becomes an essential organ of our life, performing a function which no other portion of our nature can so successfully fulfill."[5]

For many, especially in the Western world, it's not so much that the younger generation has decided not to participate in religion, it's simply that they don't consider it at all. With the many diversions provided by technology and the media, there is no time left to contemplate the enigmas of life and death. In the Katha Upanishad, "Death" says:

> "The Hereafter never rises before the thoughtless child (the ignorant), deluded by the glamour of wealth. "This world alone is, there is none other": thinking thus, he falls under my sway again and again." [6]

Religion nor philosophy can compete with social media and entertainment outlets. But unfortunately, technology cannot provide solutions to the more important philosophical concerns that must be

---

[5] William James. *The Varieties of Religious Experience: A Study in Human Nature*

[6] The Upanishads (Kindle Locations 289-290).

confronted if we are to successfully survive life. And, while these more important issues are avoided as much as possible by many, when difficult times come, when death becomes apparent, one is forced to contemplate these essential questions and search for realistic answers.

"Each night, when I go to sleep, I die. And the next morning, when I wake up, I am reborn."

— *Mahatma Gandhi*

Reincarnation: The Beginning

Maybe it's not possible to prove definitively what waits for us following this earthly life, but perhaps it is possible to show what is more reasonable and probable than any of the other options that are currently or have been historically proposed.

As I mentioned previously, a philosophy that attempts to offer an explanation of life and gives guidance for how to live life should be one that is credible. That is, it should provide evidence for its reliability. It should not be one that ignores reason. It should not be one that offers only manmade sources as proof of its validity. It should not be one that promulgates fairytale-type visions of the future with no regard for intelligence.

In other words, it should, in some way, comply with the laws of nature because these laws govern our physical universe and we, for now, are physical creatures. It should somehow be substantiated by what we know and understand in *this* life. I will discuss this aspect in more detail in later chapters.

Reincarnation sufficiently answers, consistently and credibly, life's deepest questions. It is a doctrine written over 4500 years ago as part of the Vedas, the oldest known spiritual writings that have been discovered to date. Passed down by word of mouth for centuries, they were finally written down around 1500 BCE by authors that are unknown, and in an ancient language called Sanskrit. These writings, especially the later ones called the Upanishads, now form the basis of the Hindu religion. However, adherence to the concept of rebirth does not require a person to become a Hindu or a member of any other religion. All religions contain philosophies but not all philosophies are religions. A religion is *the belief in and worship of a superhuman controlling power, especially a personal God or gods; a particular system of faith and worship.* Psychologist William James gives a good definition of religion in his lectures, *The Varieties of Religious Experience: A Study in Human Nature.* He says:

> "Religion, therefore, as I now ask you arbitrarily to take it, shall mean for us the feelings, acts, and experiences of individual men in their solitude, so far as they apprehend themselves to stand in relation to whatever they may consider the divine. Since the relation may be either moral, physical, or ritual, it is evident that out of religion in the sense in which we take it, theologies, philosophies, and ecclesiastical organizations may secondarily grow."

While Reincarnation meets the criteria of a religion, it is not a religion per se. That is, there is no organizational infrastructure and no formal statement of beliefs. It is a philosophy that goes beyond the scope of religion. It is a theory concerning God, knowledge, reality and existence.

Reincarnation is a teaching that offers a reasonable explanation for why things are the way they are, and why *we* are the way we are. As stated, there is no dogma, no prescribed ceremonies or required rituals. It is simply a philosophy that stands alone like any other philosophical theory.

As to the origin of Reincarnation, it is a mystery. William Walter Atkinson explains it this way:

"We do not believe that the doctrine of Reincarnation ever "originated" anywhere, as a new and distinct doctrine. We believe that it sprang into existence whenever and wherever man arrived at a stage of intellectual development sufficient to enable him to form a mental conception of a Something that lived after Death.

Here, then, is where the idea of Reincarnation begins—everywhere, at a certain stage of human mental development. It runs parallel with the "ghost" (spirit) idea, and seems bound up with that conception in nearly every case. When man evolves a little further, he begins to reason that if the "ghost" (spirit) is immortal, and survives the death of the body, and returns to take upon itself a new body, then it must have lived before the last birth, and therefore must have a long chain of lives behind it. This is the second step. The third step is when man begins to reason that the next life is dependent upon something done or left undone in the present life. And upon these three fundamental ideas the doctrine of Reincarnation has been built."[7]

The doctrine of Reincarnation was regarded as true to some extent by a vast number of religions around the world throughout the history of humankind. There were even those who lived in the first century, during the life of Jesus, who believed in reincarnation although it is seldom mentioned today. In Matthew 16:14 Jesus

---

[7] William Walker Atkinson. *Reincarnation and the Law of Karma / A Study of the Old-New World-Doctrine of Rebirth, and Spiritual Cause and Effect.*

asked his disciples who they thought he was. They answered:

> "Some say John the Baptist; others say Elijah; and still others, Jeremiah or one of the prophets."

Among some there was the belief that Jesus was one of those men who had died and then returned to earth, not in their original bodies, but in the body of Jesus. Many philosophers also held to the concept of rebirth.

> ☐"Pythagoras taught that the doctrine of Reincarnation accounted for the inequality observable in the lives of men on earth, giving a logical reason for the same, and establishing the fact of universal and ultimate justice, accountable for on no other grounds. He taught that although the material world was subject to the laws of destiny and fatality, yet there was another and higher state of being in which the Soul would rise above the laws of the lower world. This higher state, he taught, had laws of its own, as yet unknown to man, which tended to work out the imperfect laws of the material world, establishing harmony, ☐justice, and equality, to supply the apparent deficiencies manifested in the earth life. Following Pythagoras, Plato, the great Grecian philosopher, taught the old-new doctrine of Rebirth. He taught that the Souls of the dead must return to earth, where, in new lives, they must wear out the old earth deeds, receiving benefits for the worthy ones, and penalties for the unworthy ones, the Soul profiting by these repeated experiences, and rising step by step

toward the divine. Plato taught that the reincarnated Soul has flashes of remembrance of its former lives, and also instincts and intuitions gained by former experiences."[8]

☐ "Plato taught that in the Rebirth, the Soul was generally unconscious of its previous lives, although it may have flashes of recollection. Besides this it has a form of intuition, and innate ideas, which was believed to be the result of the experiences gained in the past lives, and which knowledge had been stored up so as to benefit the Soul in its reincarnated existence."[9]

☐ "John the Baptist was generally accepted as the reincarnation of Elias, even by the populace, who regarded it as a miraculous occurrence, while the elect regarded it as merely another instance of rebirth under the law. The Gnostics, a mystic order and school in the early church, taught Reincarnation plainly and openly, bringing upon themselves much persecution at the hands of the more conservative."[10]

In fact, the idea of reincarnation is to be found in nearly all of the philosophies and religions of the world at some period of their history. However, only in India do we see the doctrine develop fully, not only in the past but also in the present. From the earliest time, reincarnation in some form in India has been accepted. Today it is recognized by nearly all Hindus, except for the Hindu Mohammedans.

---

[8] Ibid.
[9] Ibid.
[10] Ibid.

"The teeming millions of India live and die in the full belief in Reincarnation, and to them it is accepted without a question as the only rational doctrine concerning the past, present and future of the Soul. Nowhere on this planet is there to be found such an adherence to the idea of "Soul" life—the thinking Hindu always regarding himself as a Soul occupying a body, rather than as a body "having a Soul," as so many of the Western people seem to regard themselves. And, to the Hindus, the present life is truly regarded as but one step on the stairway of life, and not as the only material life preceding an eternity of spiritual existence. To the Hindu Mind, Eternity is here with us Now—we are in eternity as much this moment as we ☐ever shall be—and the present life is but one of a number of fleeting moments in the eternal life."[11]

Because there have been so many adherents of reincarnation from a vast variety of geographical locations, the doctrine of Reincarnation has become complex and, in some cases, inconsistent. However, most of the inconsistencies occur when speculating about what happens to the Spirit between one life and another. Almost all proponents agree on the basics of how reincarnation or metempsychosis functions as an integral component in life on earth. It is my objective to address mainly this aspect of rebirth because, as mentioned previously, any talk of what occurs when we leave this life is purely speculation.

I realize that there are hundreds, perhaps thousands of individuals who profess to have memories of past lives.

---

[11] Ibid.

I will not discuss whether these are reliable or not. However, later in this thesis I will briefly discuss how near death experiences as well as testimonies of past life memories when children have been used as evidence of rebirth. I, myself, am not convinced that personal experience is permissible as evidence in an argument that requires more convincing proof. Certainly, personal experience can serve as final proof to the individual who has had the experience, but it should only be considered reliable when there is additional, non-experiential evidence. The real value of near death experiences for this study is in the context of consciousness and the brain.

If personal experience is not used as evidence for reincarnation, then what sources can we use for validation? Our main source of proof will be the laws that were incorporated into the universe by the Creator, laws to which all things must comply. These laws include: Cause and Effect (the Law of Causation), the Rule of Polarity - opposites or contraries, the scientific principle of Conservation of Energy, the Law of Attraction and the concept of Divine Justice or fairness.

The worth of Reincarnation is that it inspires character building in humans by offering a clearly reasonable reason for doing so; it encourages spiritual development—lifting humans to God rather than lowing God to humans; it illustrates how every human is responsible for their own destiny rather than being the victim of predestination. In addition, it offers a commonsense explanation for the deepest questions of life: why there is human suffering and pain; the unequal distribution of intuition, the imbalance of individual environmental conditions and other apparent inequalities; and it successfully deals with the conflict between materialism and spirituality in a way that makes sense in the real world, and, finally, it offers us the truth—as much as we can determine the truth given what we know as human beings living in a physical world—our present reality.

"Yoga says instinct is a trace of an old experience that has been repeated many times and the impressions have sunk down to the bottom of the mental lake. Although they go down, they aren't completely erased. Don't think you ever forget anything. All experiences are stored in the chittam; and, when the proper atmosphere is created, they come to the surface again. When we do something several times it forms a habit. Continue with that habit for a long time, and it becomes your character. Continue with that character and eventually, perhaps in another life, it comes up as instinct."

— *Sri S. Satchidananda*
The Yoga Sutras

Reincarnation: A Basic Understanding

The secret to understanding Reincarnation is rooted in the concept of parallel universes; that is, that there are two distinctly different, and yet tightly coalesced facets of life: one physical, the other non-physical. This is also referred to as duality. The physical (tangible) aspect of life is observable. The non-physical (intangible) aspect is unobservable. However, since we live in a world that shares both facets, it is necessary for us to have some method of understanding the unobservable, just as we do the observable, so that it does not remain a mystery.[12] The Creator has supplied us with the key to understanding. The physical universe is a reflection of the spiritual universe. Physical life is the laboratory for spiritual understanding. Many scientists will claim that there is no link between the physical and non-physical worlds—that they are distinctly different in composition and, therefore, are not relatable. However, as I will explain in subsequent chapters, the physical and the non-physical are no more than parts of a whole, and understanding one can lead us to a greater knowledge of the other.

By studying the laws and ways the physical universe operates, we are able to grasp an understanding of the spiritual universe. What better method can there be for explaining the unexplainable than by using that which *is*

---

[12] Of course, some mysteries will always exist. But through scientific discoveries, the puzzles of the natural world as well as the spiritual world are being resolved at the appropriate time. "A Science without mystery is unknown; a Religion without mystery is absurd."

explainable? Henry Drummond, in his book, *Natural Law in the Spiritual World*, says:

> "There is a sense of solidity about a Law of Nature which belongs to nothing else in the world. Here, at last, amid all that is shifting, is one thing sure; one thing outside ourselves, unbiased, unprejudiced, uninfluenced by like or dislike, by doubt or fear; one thing that holds on its way to me eternally, incorruptible, and undefiled."

> "What that discovery of Law has done for Nature, it is impossible to estimate. As a mere spectacle the universe to-day discloses a beauty so transcendent that he who disciplines himself by scientific work finds it an overwhelming reward simply to behold it. In these Laws one stands face to face with truth, solid and unchangeable. Each single Law is an instrument of scientific research, simple in its adjustments, universal in its application, infallible in its results. And despite the limitations of its sphere on every side, Law is still the largest, richest, and surest source of human knowledge."

How reasonable it is for the Creator to have designed into the physical world the keys to unlocking the mysteries of the non-physical world. With every scientific discovery we solve another enigma of the physical universe and of the non-physical as well. Not that the natural laws of this world are applicable to the spiritual dimension, but that by understanding how one operates, we are given insights as to how the other functions. For instance, just as there is physical evolution, there is spiritual evolution. Both are intended to transport its object to the ideal state; the best it can be: perfection.

We should begin by defining a few terms in order to clarify how they will be used in this discourse.

1. While there are numerous definitions for what constitutes life, we will use one that is simple and widely accepted by a general audience: *for something to be a living organism it must be able to grow and reproduce itself.*

2. By the term "physical" I am referring to the *materialistic, tangible and matter-oriented aspect of life.*

3. "Spiritual" is a very ambiguous term. For the purposes of this discourse, I am using it to mean *the nonphysical, intangible aspect of existence.* I am not necessarily referring to the association of man to any spiritual being unless specifically noted. Where I use the term *spiritual evolution*, I am not referring to a person becoming more "holy". I am referring to an individual developing a life that is less focused on material assets.

So, what do I mean when I use the term reincarnation?

William Atkinson offers an excellent overview of Reincarnation:

> "By "Reincarnation" we mean the repeated incarnation, or embodiment in flesh, of the Soul or immaterial part of man's nature. The term "Metempsychosis" is frequently employed in the same sense, the definition of the latter term being: "The passage of the Soul, as an immortal

essence, at the death of the body, into another living body."

Atkinson goes on to explain that another term used by some, more primitive races in connection with reincarnation is "Trans-migration of Souls"; this term being used in the sense of "passing from one body into another". This belief held that the Souls of men sometimes returned in the form of lower animals as punishment for sins committed during their human life. However, this belief is not a part of contemporary Reincarnation doctrine as this idea originated from an entirely different source and therefore has nothing in common with Metempsychosis. In the course of spiritual evolution, this evolving is always a process of moving forward, never backward. A fully conscious creature will not revert to one of less consciousness. I discuss this more fully in future chapters.

Atkinson continues in his explanation of contemporary Reincarnation:

> "This fundamental belief may be expressed as the doctrine that there is in man an immaterial Something (called the Soul, spirit, inner self, or many other names) which does not perish at the death or disintegration of the body, but which persists as an entity, and after a shorter or longer interval of rest reincarnates, or is re-born, into a new body—that of an unborn infant—from whence it proceeds to live a new life in the body, more or less unconscious of its past existences, but containing within itself the "essence" or results of its past lives, which experiences go to make up its new "character," or "personality." It is usually held that the

> rebirth is governed by the Law of Attraction, under one name or another, and which law operates in accordance with strict justice, in the direction of attracting the reincarnating Soul to a body, and conditions, in accordance with the tendencies of the past life, the parents also attracting to them a Soul bound to them by some ties in the past, the law being universal, uniform, and equitable to all concerned in the matter."[13]

E. D. Walker, a well-known English writer gives the further insight into the idea of the general teachings:

> "Reincarnation teaches that the Soul enters this life, not as a fresh creation, but after a long course of previous existences on this earth and elsewhere, in which it acquired its present inhering peculiarities, and that it is on the way to future transformations which the Soul is now shaping. It claims that infancy brings to earth, not a blank scroll for the beginning of an earthly record, nor a mere cohesion of atomic forces into a brief personality, soon to dissolve again into the elements, but that it is inscribed with ancestral histories, some like the present scene, most of them unlike it and stretching back into the remotest past. These inscriptions are generally undecipherable, save as revealed in their molding influence upon the new career; but like the invisible photographic images made by the sun of all it sees, when they are properly developed in the laboratory of consciousness they will be distinctly displayed. The current phase of life will also be stored away in the

---

[13] Ibid.

> secret vaults of memory, for its unconscious effects upon the ensuing lives. All the qualities we now possess, in body, Mind and Soul, result from our use of ancient opportunities. We are indeed 'the heir of all the ages,' and are alone ☐responsible for our inheritances. For these conditions accrue from distant causes engendered by our older selves, and the future flows by the divine law of cause and effect from the gathered momentum of our past impetuses. There is no favoritism in the universe, but all have the same everlasting facilities for growth."

What does this mean? It means that in order to grow spiritually, we must face the challenges that will provide us with the best opportunities for growth. Those who were elevated to a prestigious position in the present life might find themselves experiencing very humble surroundings in the next. The wealthy might be poor. The diligent worker in this life is preparing his life for greatness in the next. I believe it was Jesus who is credited with saying, " the last shall be first and the first last".[14] Hardships give rise to strength, suffering teaches patience, self-denial develops will. Every experience is one of value, whether we recognize it or not.

> "Tastes cultivated in this existence will somehow bear fruit in coming ones; and acquired energies will assert themselves whenever they can by the Law of Parsimony[15]

---

[14] Matthew 20:16 KJV

[15] The Law of Parsimony, also called the principle of economy, is the principle that the simplest explanation of an event or observation is the preferred explanation. Simplicity is understood in various ways, including the requirement that an explanation should (a) make the smallest number

upon which the principles of physics are based. Vice versa, the unconscious habits, the uncontrollable impulses, the peculiar tendencies, the favorite pursuits, and the Soul-stirring friendships of the present descend from far-reaching previous activities.[16]

"It is argued that only by repeated incarnations the soul is able to realize the futility of the search for happiness and satisfaction in material things. One, while dissatisfied and disappointed at his own condition, is apt to imagine that in some other earthly condition he would find satisfaction and happiness now denied him, and dying carries with him the subconscious desire to enjoy those conditions, which desire attracts him back to earth-life in search of those conditions. So long as the soul desires anything that earth can offer, it is earth-bound and drawn back into the vortex. But after repeated incarnations the soul learns well its lesson that only in itself may be found happiness—and that only when it learns its real nature, source, and destiny—and then it passes on to higher planes.

"Along this same line it is urged that the soul's development must come largely from contact and relationship with other souls, in a variety of phases and forms. It must experience pain and happiness, love, pity, failure, success—it must know the discipline of sympathy, toleration,

---

of unsupported assumptions, (b) postulate the existence of the fewest entities, and (c) invoke the fewest unobservable constructs.

[16] William Walker Atkinson. *Reincarnation and the Law of Karma / A Study of the Old-New World-Doctrine of Rebirth, and Spiritual Cause and Effect.*

patience, energy, fortitude, foresight, gratitude, pity, benevolence, and love in all of its phases. This, it is urged, is possible only through repeated incarnations, as the span of one life is too small and its limit too narrow to embrace but a small fraction of the necessary experiences of the soul on its journey toward development and attainment."[17]

So, how does Reincarnation fit into the 21st century and beyond? What does this ancient doctrine hold for us today?

---

[17] Ibid.

"As a caterpillar, having come to the end of one blade of grass, draws itself together and reaches out for the next, so the Self, having come to the end of one life and dispelled all ignorance, gathers in his faculties and reaches out from the old body to a new."

*— The Brihadaranyaka
Upanishad IV.4.3*

Reincarnation and the Laws of the Universe

The universe is constructed in the most remarkable fashion. Every aspect of its design and operation appears to be carefully and meticulously planned down to the finest detail. To reiterate a previously made point, while the observable material universe holds many mysteries, it also serves to unlock many unobservable, spiritual mysteries. If we examine the laws and principals of nature, we can draw a comparison or a parallel between the two. Earlier I used the example of physical evolution. Physical evolution occurs slowly and has as its goal the progressive development of substances from their most basic form to their most perfect form. Similarly, spiritual evolution is a gradual process where a Spirit, or Soul, is transformed from a primitive, dualistic entity into a perfect God-like Soul. This physical/spiritual analogy provides us with a method for unlocking the enigmas of spiritual existence.

As we delve into the meaning of what has been said about Reincarnation in the previous pages, we need to understand how Metempsychosis complies with the Laws of the Universe. These laws exist to provide order to the universe and offer us a method for unlocking the mysteries of how our physical universe functions. The four main Universal Laws that we will be concerned with are the Law of Polarity, the Law of Cause and Effect, the Law of Conservation of Energy and the Principal of Attraction.

The Law of Cause and Effect is basically easy to understand. Where there is an action, there is a reaction or a series of reactions—or consequences. However, the

Law of Cause and Effect can seem somewhat complicated in that every cause is an effect and every effect becomes a cause. Let me explain. Let's suppose that I give medicine to a person who is ill. I am the cause of the person having the medicine. The person takes the medicine (cause) and gets well (effect). Because the person gets well (cause) they are able to go back to work (effect). And so on. Every cause may result in many effects (consequences), each effect branches out as the cause of many other effects. In other words, the cycle of cause and effect is endless.

Furthermore, it seems that in some instances, the cause is also affected by the effect. Or, put another way, there is a consequence for every action, a consequence that travels in both directions: away from the instigator of the action toward others and a consequence that returns to the instigator in the form of positive or negative vibrations. This is where Divine Justice comes into play. We will discuss this in a later chapter.

The Law of Conservation of Energy (The First Law of Thermodynamics) simply states that energy cannot be created or destroyed. We will delve more into this law and how it applies to Reincarnation in a later chapter.

The Law of Polarity is also called the Law of Opposites or Contraries. Primary examples of opposites are light and dark, happy and sad, rich and poor, and up and down. For every quality and value there is an opposite one. In fact, nothing would not and could not have identity whatsoever if not for its very opposite. Because of these opposites, we can say that we live in a dualistic world where opposites are constantly in opposition or in conflict with one another---love and hate, hot and cold, physical and spiritual. This is where things do get a little confusing because even though these are opposing values, since both are essential for making the other possible, we can conclude that together these opposites form a unique unity; a unity that consists of a pair of values that are opposite but where one is completely dependent for the existence of the other. Where one exists, the other must also be present in order to form a whole or unified oneness.

Therefore, we live in a dualistic world where opposite values actually complement each other to form a whole. While these opposites always exist, they are not always equal in value. If they were, they would create a stasis or equilibrium absent of movement. So, as values adjust—one increasing the other decreasing, the balance shifts between the two. Imagine a bar with a pole at each end. On one end is the value, "hot" and on the other, the value, "cold".

Each pole at extreme ends of the bar represents absolute temperature hot and cold, a value that can never be achieved. However, as the value "hot" moves along the bar toward the value, "cold", it decreases in temperature. Finally, if it moves close enough to the opposite pole, "cold", it retains no measurable heat at all.

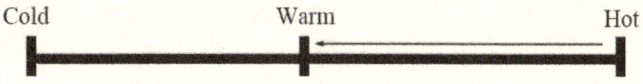

If we replace the words "hot" and "cold" with the words "physical" and "spiritual" (non-physical) we can easily visualize how duality functions in our life.

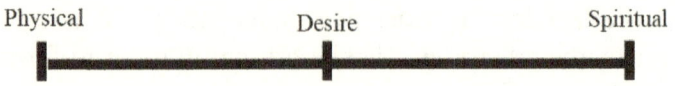

Socrates[18] explained it this way: when one absolute value is impacted by its opposite value, it no longer retains its original value. It becomes something less than what it was. Hot affected by cold is no longer hot, but some lesser degree of that value; perhaps warm. Likewise, as we move further away from desiring physical things and set our will on spiritual things, we move the scale away from the physical and toward its opposite—the spiritual, until the physical has no influence on us at all. In this case, when one value totally dominates, eliminating its opposite, duality disappears and there is complete unity. That is the ultimate goal of Reincarnation. When materialism no longer has any influence and the spiritual dominates our minds completely, we have achieved perfection: unity with the spirit.

> ☐"When certain powers predominate they manifest first while the others remain dormant. As we find in the process of evolution, when animal nature manifests perfectly the moral and spiritual nature remain latent. Again when moral and spiritual nature manifest fully, the animal is in abeyance. It is for this reason we do not find expressions of moral and spiritual nature in

---

[18] Plato. *Phaedo*.

> lower animals or in those human beings who live like them. Man is the only animal in whom such perfect expressions of moral and spiritual nature are possible. When the individual soul begins to study its spiritual nature, its lower or animal nature is gradually eclipsed. As the higher nature becomes powerful the lower nature dwindles into insignificance; its energy is transformed into that of the higher nature, and ultimately it disappears altogether and rises no more. Then the soul becomes free from the lower or animal nature."[19]

These laws or principles are active in the universe and they impact every aspect of life. Everything that exists, as we know it, is subject to these basic principles. Once we grasp these four laws, we can begin to understand how Reincarnation operates in accordance with these rules.

> "There is, then, this Spirit of Infinite Life and Power behind all which is the source of all. This Infinite Power is creating, working, ruling through the agency of great immutable laws and forces that run through all the universe, that surround us on every side. Every act of our every-day lives is governed by these same great laws and forces. Every flower that blooms by the wayside, springs up, grows, ☐blooms, fades, according to certain great immutable laws. Every snowflake that plays between earth and heaven, forms, falls, melts, according to certain great unchangeable laws. In a sense there is nothing in all the great universe but law. If this

---

[19] Swami Abhedananda. *Five Lectures on Reincarnation.*

is true there must of necessity be a force behind it all that is the maker of these laws and a force greater than the laws that are made."[20]

Why is this important? It is important because these laws are consistent throughout our universe—our present reality. This world and its processes are all that we know—all that we can know for certain. By functioning in accordance with Universal Laws, Reincarnation helps us understand the relationship between life and death, and how to successfully apply these concepts and philosophies to our physical life while at the same time, developing our spirituality. It helps us unlock many of the mysteries that hold us hostage to ignorance. Reincarnation is the only life/death philosophy that enables us to understand our dualistic composition and, therefore, comprehend how our spiritual life affects our physical existence and vice-versa. The present and the future are no longer mysteries. In other words, life makes sense.

---

[20] Ralph Waldo Trine. *In Tune with the Infinite; or, Fullness of Peace, Power, and Plenty.*

"We know that Hinduism believes in reincarnation. Such beliefs or theories have one purpose. It is to provide a plausible answer to our questions that would otherwise remain unanswered. We have questions such as, "Why should I perform work if the result is not likely to be seen; especially when death can visit me at any moment? And then: Why should death happen at all? And why do our kith and kin have to be engulfed in grief when we die? Is it not injustice and something not acceptable?" The Gita tries to assuage such feelings by stating that just as we attain childhood, youth, and old age, similarly, we also attain another body after our death. It is a continuous and cyclical process, and the wise ones should not have worries in this regard."

— *Nihar Satpathy,*
The Puzzles of Life

God and the Soul

As I mentioned previously, there are two fundamental truths that form the foundation of Reincarnation: the existence of a supernatural entity,[21] and the presence of an individual immortal component that we will call a Soul or Spirit.

Most people who are engaged in some religious organization already believe in the existence of these two entities. However, because these are fundamental to Reincarnation, I feel it necessary to spend some time discussing the reasonableness of their existence.

So, our initial question is, can we prove that these two entities exist if their essence is non-physical?

The question of the existence of a god or divine being has been argued for thousands of years by the greatest minds that have lived. The goal of most of these arguments was to somehow prove, definitively or absolutely, that such an entity exists or that it doesn't. However, we must agree that if this Being is beyond our physical world, that is, that it is not limited to those laws of nature that limit us like time and space, nor is it made of matter, then we have little chance of proving or disproving its existence simply because it is beyond our comprehension. Since we are limited by these laws, we can only understand and conceive of the things that are like us—things that are within our experience and observation. On the other hand, as stated earlier, if we utilize reason and commonsense to determine if it is more reasonable to believe that such an entity exists

---

[21] This Entity goes by many names: God, Allah, Brahman, Self, Yahweh, etc.

than that it doesn't, we should be able to conclude one way or the other and feel confident that with the information we have at this time, we have come close to realizing the truth concerning the existence of these entities.

So, we will begin with the most basic question: does some kind of supernatural entity actually exist? Is there a God?

In regard to the existence of God, we have two options:

- There is no God and we are the product of chance and evolution by natural selection alone. Consequently, the meaning of life is survival and our purpose is to enjoy life as much as we can here and now since death is the end of our existence.

- There is a supernatural entity of some kind who has utilized evolution to execute a plan or design for the creation and development of the universe and everything in it. In this case, meaning and purpose become a little more difficult to determine, but it implies that there is a reason for our existence.

So, how can we determine what is true concerning the existence of God? Where can we look for reasonable evidence?

"Reincarnation isn't something in which I choose to believe but rather a truth I accept. Most people will never know the meaning of their friendships, passions, choices and even challenges. I embrace them, knowing that there's always a perfect correlation between everything, including between us and the ones that love us and betray us at the end. That's how I know I'm almost never traveling somewhere but returning, or not meeting someone but fixing the past, or facing a challenge but ending a karmic cycle. If I was a Buddhist Monk, a Scottish Doctor, a French Monarch, or a Spanish Templar, none of that really matters, not as much as what I experienced and believed during that time, not as much as what I did ten years ago or what I believed during my childhood, not as much as who I am now and what I can do with my life at present time."

— *Robin Sacredfire*

Does God Exist?

I have included this section for skeptics such as myself that are still trying to find an answer to that all-important question concerning God. Several years ago, I set out to discover for myself once and for all if God exists. I embarked on that journey realizing that many others more intelligent than I have made this conquest a lifelong mission, and most have ended without resolution. It was not my intent, however, to prove definitively if a supernatural entity exists, but rather if it is more reasonable to believe that one exists than it is to believe that one does not exist. My main criterion for the search was to maintain an open mind, ready to accept whatever conclusion the evidence supported. Based on the following observations and commonsense reasoning, I am now a firm believer in a supernatural entity that created the world in which we live.

On the contrary, for many people the question of the existence of God is satisfactorily settled without evidence or credible substantiation. The determinant might have been a sensation or an intuition or a particular type of experience. But once accepted as authentic, these impressions pointed to an entity that became a reality without the aid of concrete evidence. This fact was an observation of the great psychologist and philosopher William James.

> "The truth is that in the metaphysical and religious sphere, articulate reasons are cogent for us only when our inarticulate feelings of reality have already been impressed in favor of the same conclusion.

> Our impulsive belief is here always what sets up the original body of truth, and our articulately verbalized philosophy is but its showy translation into formulas. The unreasoned and immediate assurance is the deep thing in us, the reasoned ☐argument is but a surface exhibition. Instinct leads, intelligence does but follow."[22]

However, for others of us who are not so easily convinced, I offer my findings and conclusions. As I have said, it should be obvious that there's not a way to prove, absolutely, that God exists or doesn't exist.[23] When I discuss the existence of God it's important to keep in mind that I'm not referring to the gods that have been granted human characteristics as portrayed throughout history by the various mythologies and religions. I'm referring to a supernatural entity that exists beyond the realm of human understanding. After all, how can we even begin to conceive of a being that is powerful enough to create the universe and exist everywhere at once?

Often times when people discuss the existence of a deity, they get bogged down in discussing the perceived nature of the deity or how religion has impacted civilization. If we are going to discuss the existence or non-existence of this entity, we must initially clear away all preconceived notions of what this deity is like and how society has used or abused their understanding of it. We must focus solely on whether or not it exists.

---

[22] William James. *The Varieties of Religious nExperience; A Study in Human Nature.* Longmans, Green, and Co. 1917.
[23] The following segment regarding the existence of God is taken from my book, *Are We Being Deceived.* Amazon

Throughout the history of human consciousness mankind has been captivated by nature and the universe. As it turns out, the more we learn about nature, the more we learn about ourselves. In fact, there are those who believe that nature holds the answers to all of life's questions—that there are no mysteries that cannot be solved if we examine the processes, natural laws and workings of the universe. So that's where we will begin.

Great men throughout history have championed the logic of an Intelligent Designer. Some might claim that those who argued for the existence of God using the cosmological argument failed to succeed in winning their argument, and that the universe does not provide credible evidence of the existence of such an entity. On the contrary, they did not fail, their message was drowned out by those who claimed to have had a more scientific solution to creation. Most of those who have tried to disprove the existence of a Creator have used evolution as proof that an intelligent power did not create the world. But evolution actually serves as evidence for such a Creator. Once again, it's important to remember that as we look for truth, whether it is scientific or religious, we will use objective evidence to substantiate our propositions. Once we have substantiated our propositions, we will attempt to formulate a conclusion. If our conclusion meets the criteria that we have established for truth and it agrees with reality, then we must presume that our conclusion is valid. The conclusion, then, becomes what we might call the accepted fact or truth about that issue until which time more information becomes available and our theory is modified to reflect the impact of that new information. This new information can then either further substantiate our theory or disprove the theory all together. The fact is that almost everything we believe is, in truth, a theory, always subject to reevaluation based on new information and discoveries.

Almost all of our current theories were originally based on observation and common sense. We must always begin there. In ancient times, people observed that the sun rose and traveled from horizon to horizon. It made sense to assume that the sun revolved around the earth. That assumption was considered the truth until new discoveries forced a change to the theory. Now we know that the earth rotates around the sun. This new information brought us closer to the truth. However, it began with common sense and observation. That's where we will begin. We will build our argument by considering the information that is available to us on the particular issue that we are discussing and employ logic and reason to formulate a theory. We will build our argument using certain ground rules. As I have mentioned, when discussing the existence or nonexistence of a supernatural being we must remember that it is just that, supernatural. If a deity does exist, then it is otherworldly—it is beyond human understanding and is not bound by the limitations of this world. In other words, it is not human—not a physical being. If it is not a physical being and it is otherworldly then it is not restricted to the scientific boundaries and physical laws of this world. It is not limited by time and space. It is not made of matter and, therefore, does not have to follow the rules that apply to matter. Initially, we must not attribute any characteristics to this entity if it exists. Once again, if it is not human, it does not necessarily possess any of the traits or attributes that humans do such as compassion or jealousy or greed or any other such characteristics. This entity must remain incomprehensible. Remember, the original question is not what is God, or who is God or what is God like. The original question is: is it more reasonable and logical and does it make more sense to believe that such a being exists than that it doesn't.

We should begin with the basic question: where did everything come from? Where did our universe originate given what we know?

We should begin with what we know, or what is proposed by science at the writing of this thesis. The most popular scientific theory is that the universe as we know it began with the "Big Bang".

> "The Big Bang Theory is the leading explanation for how the universe began. Simply put, it says the universe as we know it started with an infinitely hot and dense single point that inflated and stretched — first at unimaginable speeds, and then at a more measurable rate — over the next 13.7 billion years to the still-expanding cosmos that we know today.
>
> "Suddenly, an explosive expansion began, ballooning our universe outwards faster than the speed of light. This was a period of cosmic inflation that lasted mere fractions of a second — about 10^{-32} of a second, according to physicist Alan Guth's 1980 theory that changed the way we think about the Big Bang forever.
>
> "When cosmic inflation came to a sudden and still-mysterious end, the more classic descriptions of the Big Bang took hold. A flood of matter and radiation, known as "reheating,"

began populating our universe with the stuff we know today: particles, atoms, the stuff that would become stars and galaxies and so on."[24]

While the Big Bang is the most popular theory concerning the beginning of the universe at this time, we need to go back before that event. We'll begin with the assumption that nothing comes from nothing. So, the Big Bang didn't just happen, something had to cause the Big Bang to bang. If there was nothing before the "bang" then there was nothing to cause the bang. In fact, there could not even have been empty space because there would have needed to have been a cause for space. Remember, nothing comes from nothing. So the question remains, what was there at the very beginning that started it all? It had to be something that existed from the infinite past. That "something" is what some people call the First Cause; something that has always existed and was the original cause of all things, something that didn't come from nothing because it always existed.

This "something" could not have been the universe, itself, because science tells us that our universe had a beginning. It could not have been space because space is nothing more than a void. If something existed in space then it, too, would have had to have always existed. And we know that empty space, being void of all elements or substances could never have led to the birth of the universe because empty space is just empty space. It could not have been atoms because atoms are made up of three elements: protons, neutrons and electrons. So these three elements would have had to

---

[24] Space.com – *The Universe; What is the Big Bang Theory?* – By Elizabeth Howell, Andrew May – Updated July 26, 2023

have always existed as well. If this were true we would be saying that there was not one single always-existent entity, but three. Additionally, these were supposedly created during the Big Bang.

This leaves us with two options. The first is that whatever it was that existed is an unknown; some particle or substance; some matter that has yet to be discovered that was present in the beginning but is no longer identifiable; or, secondly, that there is an entity that has always existed that is not matter that is capable of creating something out of nothing. With our sophisticated laboratories and advanced scientific capabilities, it is not reasonable to assume that such a particle or substance exists or existed that we have not been able to identify. The second option, and the most logical and reasonable, is that this ever-existent entity is non-matter and that it has the power to create something out of nothing—The First Cause; but what kind of non-matter?

Again, according to science, the Big Bang was caused by the universe experiencing an incredible burst of expansion called "inflation". But what caused this inflation? Through years of research and the use of powerful telescopes they discovered that something is pushing the galaxies apart in the universe.

> "Something, not like matter and not like ordinary energy, is pushing the galaxies apart. This 'stuff' has been dubbed 'dark energy' but to give it a name is not to understand it. Whether dark energy is a type of dynamical fluid, heretofore unknown to physics, or whether it is a property of the vacuum of empty space, or

whether it is some modification to general relativity is not yet known."²⁵

Energy is everywhere. It is the force that causes things to happen in the universe. Einstein predicted that empty space can possess its own energy.

> "The Latin phrase "creatio ex nihilo" means "creation out of nothing," and it's largely the domain of theology, philosophy and mythology for a reason: the first law of thermodynamics, which is actually a conservation of energy equation. The gist of that equation, as you no doubt remember, is that energy can neither be created nor destroyed.
>
> "To manufacture matter in a way that adheres to the first law of thermodynamics, you have to convert energy into matter. This conversion occurred on a cosmic scale about 13 billion years ago. The big bang consisted entirely of energy. Matter only came into being as rapid cooling occurred."²⁶

So, perhaps some kind of energy was the First Cause since the natural law of energy conservation states that energy can neither be created nor destroyed.

Now I'll move on to my next point and I'll return to this argument momentarily. Let's continue by discussing how life originated. The law of Cause and Effect tells us that there is a cause for every effect. So, we must assume that something that existed before the Big Bang, or as a result of it is responsible for the origination of life. While there are many theories, there are only a few

---

[25] *The Big Bang.* science.nasa.gov
[26] Robert Lamb. *Can We Manufacture Matter?* Howstuffworks.com

that are popular with a general and scientific audience. Creationism, Intelligent Design, and the Anthropic Principle are three; the fourth is the theory that claims that over time life evolved from nonliving matter. We'll call that Spontaneous Generation. For the moment, I will combine Creationism and Intelligent Design because they both credit an intelligent entity with the creation of life and the world. Let's take a look at these various theories briefly and logically.

Like all theories concerning the existence of sapient life, the Anthropic Principle is very confusing even within the field of science. In a nutshell, the Anthropic Principle suggests that there are many planets, perhaps billions and billions in the universe and of these planets there are many that are probably friendly to life. That is, they would be life-friendly if life existed on them. And because of this favorable environment, somewhere at some time, life simply appeared. It theorizes that life just popped up because the conditions were conducive for life to exist. That's very much like saying if you build a road that is conducive to automobile travel, an automobile will eventually come, without stating how or why it appeared other than because there was a suitable place for it. It is not a very popular theory among most scientists.

Probably the most popular theory is the assumption that over time, nonliving matter somehow came together in a primordial soup that resulted in a living organism. But what evidence is there to support this theory? While much experimentation has been done and is still being done today, even with our sophisticated laboratories, scientists have not been able to produce life from nonliving substances. As far as we know from actual historical data, there are no examples that clearly offer proof that such a process has ever occurred.[27]

Simply put, the proponents of this theory, propose that life appeared as a matter of chance. They suggest that over time the necessary chemicals, having been produced as a result of the changing environment, mixed and mingled together and that this combining of chemicals resulted in the creation of the basic building blocks of life. And, eventually, over time, these building blocks became a living organism. At this time, there is no evidence at all to support this theory. We have to remember that life is more than a chemical reaction. It involves complex systems and processes. In fact, there are seven characteristics of a living substance: it takes in nourishment, it is capable of movement, it breathes, it excretes, it grows, it possesses sensitivity and it reproduces. One of the most accepted definitions of life is the ability of an organism to grow and reproduce itself. Even in a very primitive organism, these capabilities or processes could not have evolved over time. They must have existed in the first living organism, even though it might have been a very primitive system. These processes are essential for sustaining life.

There are other problems with this theory. If life did originate through a slow chemical process, did it occur only in one place with one organism being produced, or in several places with many organisms produced of slightly varying kinds? If it occurred in several places,

---

[27] In 2010, scientists from 3 universities built the first single-celled synthetic organism but it was not built completely from scratch. Instead they started with previously existing simple-type living bacteria called a mycoplasma. Reference: NIST.com- *Scientists Create Simple Synthetic Cell That Grows and Divides Normally*. March 29, 2021.

the odds of such a chance meeting of just the right chemicals in just the right environment to create this new life are even more overwhelming.

As mentioned, there are simply no examples of life coming from non-living substances in nature. On the other hand, there is ample evidence of non-living substances having come from living things. Fossils were living organisms that died and became solid matter. Also, there are petrified, stone-like objects that were the result of the demise of living organisms and substances. And we should add that it has been shown that many of our natural resources such as oil and gas and coal were also the result of decaying organisms. So, there is ample evidence of non-living matter coming from living things, but no evidence at all of living organisms being created by non-living matter or as a result of some chemical reaction. Furthermore, we have significant evidence of living organisms coming from living organisms. This is called Biogenesis. Every living thing reproduces.

So if we agree that life only comes naturally from life, based on observation and experience, and we see that life can produce non-living substances, then we must conclude that the First Cause was some kind of life form.

So, as stated, in the beginning we have some form of energy and we have life. But life, itself, is a form of energy. Therefore it is conceivable, even probable, that this unknown energy that existed in the beginning was life—life that caused the Big Bang, life that created matter and life that created life.

Now that we have discussed the creation of life, we will turn to evolution to substantiate our theory. Many people see a conflict between creation by design and science. Obviously, I am not among those. If God is the creator of all things, then God is the creator of science and all of the other disciplines. If this is true then the more information we have concerning life and our universe, the more evidence there should be to support the theory that there is a Supreme Existence that has carefully and intelligently orchestrated the creation of the universe. Science can help us in our quest for understanding.

Of course, the most popular theory of evolution is Darwin's theory of evolution by natural selection delineated in his book, *The Origen of Species*.

Traditionally, it is taught that Darwin believed that evolution was the result of natural selection exclusively. But, according to his own words, Darwin is not arguing against the participation of a Supreme Creator in his book. What he is arguing against is the idea of the creation of each species being an independent act without the aid of evolutionary involvement. He says believing that theory,

> "…makes the works of God a mere mockery and deception; I would almost as soon believe with the old and ignorant cosmogonists, that fossil shells had never lived, but had been created in stone so as to mock the shells now living on the sea-shore."[28]

Even Darwin believed in the hand of God in creation. In fact, on several occasions he refers to a Creator.

There are other theories that are still being argued. And, there are still many holes that must be filled in all

---

[28] Charles Darwin, *The Origin of Species*, Gramercy Press. P. 202

theories concerning evolution. Even Darwin admitted that. He had trouble explaining the evolution of such organs as the eyes. In *Origin of Species* he says,

> "To suppose that the eye, with all its inimitable contrivances for adjusting the focus to different distances, for admitting different amounts of light, and for the correction of spherical and chromatic aberration could have been formed by natural selection, seems, I freely confess, absurd in the highest possible degree."[29]

He then continues to explain some of the ways that these complicated organs could have developed, realizing all the while that his suppositions were strictly speculation. But, let me point out the difficulties with the development of these organs strictly on the basis of natural selection. In his book, *Darwin's Black Box*, Dr. Michael J. Behe, a professor of Biological Science at Lehigh University, calls such complex systems as sight and sound "irreducibly complex". Here's the way he explains it:

> "By irreducibly complex I mean a single system composed of several well-matched, interacting parts that contribute to the basic function, wherein the removal of any one of the parts causes the system to effectively cease functioning. An irreducibly complex system cannot be produced directly (that is, by continuously improving the initial function, which continues to work by the same mechanism) by slight, successive modifications of a precursor system, because any precursor to an irreducibly complex system that is missing a

---

[29] Ibid., p. 217.

part is by definition nonfunctional . . . Since natural selection can only choose systems that are already working, then if a biological system cannot be produced gradually it would have to arise as an integrated unit, in one fell swoop, for natural selection to have anything to act on."[30]

Additionally, if an organism exists and has always existed in a world of darkness and silence, surviving and living successfully in that environment, even in the face of competition and changing conditions, then there is no logical reason for the development of such organs that produce sight and sound. Consider, in addition, with the appearance of that new organ, the eye for instance, the organism not only had to develop the physical eye with its complex retina, but also had to simultaneously develop an entirely new support system of nerves uniquely designed to collect the various intensities of light, convert the light to electrical impulses and communicate those impulses to a part of the brain that was capable of identifying that data and turning that information into images. The theory that this organ, with all of these unique nerves, and a brain that could translate this information into sight all occurring by chance, over time and yet congruently, is illogical. Especially given that the organism was already surviving without this capability. Certainly, adaptations like fins or other appendages that would help an organism to move more quickly would give them an advantage over the competition, but sight and hearing, having not been present in any previously existent organism, would not have been a "natural" progression necessary for survival. This same argument

---

[30] Michael J. Behe, *Darwin's Black Box,* (Free Press, NY, 2006), 39

holds true for the development of all vital organs. As I mentioned, if evolution is mainly concerned with survival, then an organism with an already functioning system would not need to have that system modified, that is to say, not drastically modified.

And, along that same line of thought, if these modifications did occur slowly over time with the essential support systems being developed deliberately for their eventual use as part of some complex system, then something, somewhere had to know what the end result of this development would be. Something had to dictate how all of the parts would fit together in order to accomplish the final objective—that of hearing or seeing. Who knew that sight would be needed? Who knew that wings would be needed? Did evolution make these decisions? If we credit evolution with these intelligent designs we are simply saying that evolution is an intelligent creative supernatural entity. We are calling evolution, God.

Finally, if evolution is mainly concerned with survival, then we should ask, what creature has the best assurance of survival: one that is unisexual, possessing a male or female reproductive organ only, or one that is hermaphroditic, one that possesses both reproductive organs and can reproduce by itself without a mate? Logically, the one that has the best chance for survival would be the one that is self-sufficient—that could reproduce on its own, guaranteeing the survival of the species. So why was there a gender split—male and female? And how did this occur? If this split occurred as a mutation, chances are it would not have been able to reproduce itself, or it would have reproduced a mix of hermaphroditic and gender-specific individuals. And, if it were a mutation, it probably would have become extinct given that there were no available mates. Now, even though it is illogical, let's suppose that this is what happened, that there was this gender split as a part of some mutation. Seeing that virtually all organisms have male and female gender, it means that this mutation not only occurred in one species, but in almost all of the species that exist today. What are the chances of that happening? So, the gender that survived would actually be the mutation that should not have survived due to the complexity of finding a mate to reproduce. And, of course, most mutations cannot reproduce at all. Therefore, it is not logical that the development of genders occurred as a part of natural selection since natural selection is concerned with what works best for survival. The appearance of gender is one of the strongest arguments against a system of natural selection as the only means of evolution.

Once again, in *The Origin of Species,* Darwin observes that only those adaptations that benefited the survival of the organism became permanent in that organism.

> "Natural selection will never produce in a being anything injurious to itself, for natural selection acts solely by and for the good of each. No organ will be formed, as Paley has remarked, for the purpose of causing pain or for doing an injury to its possessor."[31]

Knowing this, we have to ask, how possible is it that adaptations and variations—not just in one organism, but a myriad of organisms, were beneficial one hundred percent of the time if we attribute those modifications to chance? Where in history or science do we have an

---

[31] Darwin, p. 229.

example that illustrates how chance produces only positive results one hundred percent of the time? Conversely, it is simple to illustrate how chance cannot produce consistent results. Let's use an example. Let's suppose we have 5 dice and we throw those dice 10 times. What are the odds that all of the dice will result in the same number all ten times? Now, multiply the number of dice a thousand times, to represent each organism affected by natural selection and all of the aspects of nature that work together harmoniously and interdependently providing the perfect environment for life, and try to calculate the odds of that occurring by chance. Chance is not consistent or dependable. Chance is random. Chance is about odds, and the odds that chance will result in a predictable and positive outcome 100% of the time is illogical, unreasonable and does not conform to reality. Just ask anyone who has visited a casino and played a game of 'chance'.

And, finally we must consider the evolution of humans. Why are we humans the only creatures with a higher level of development—consciously, intellectually, psychologically and emotionally? Certainly, there were a many other creatures that evolved in the same areas that humans did—in the same environment, under the same conditions. Why didn't they, too, evolve in similar ways as humans? Shouldn't there be a species of tiger that can talk and think and use logic to make decisions? Shouldn't a bear be sitting at the United Nations debating global warming? Why were humans the only ones to reach this pinnacle of development? Why were we the only ones whose brain grew and developed such capabilities as we have today?

The current problem is a problem of objectivity. It appears that once science has adopted a theory that it wants to believe, it will go to any length to prove that theory is true even when there is evidence to the contrary. Additionally, many experts and scientists are so focused on their own particular discipline that they tend to develop tunnel vision, seeing their specialization as the only science that matters. However, if we take a step back and look at all of nature as one elaborate, multifaceted body, we can easily recognize that each area of science is no more than a part of the whole. If we examine astronomy, we can easily see the tremendous order of the universe. Can chance ever lead to anything but chaos? Can chance result in consistent seasons, invariable tides, in planets that remain, century after century, confined to their specific orbits, each affecting the movement of the others? Can the earth, sun and moon be positioned by chance so that we have light and warmth part of the day and cool darkness the other? If we consider behavioral science and recognize the wonder of cause and effect and other natural universal laws, and how these laws bring order to the world; and if we add to that the examination of evolution, we cannot help but acknowledge the tremendous order and design of all things. Coincidence? There are far too many occurrences to be coincidence or chance. The odds against it are far too great. All of these aspects of nature, logically and reasonably, cannot have been accidental, but the perfect design of an indescribable, incomprehensible, intelligent, creative existence. Any other option is illogical.

In conclusion, we are left with two clues concerning the creation of the universe that has been given to us by science and reason. The first is that before the Big Bang there existed a unique type of energy. The second is that before there was life on earth there existed some kind of life that was responsible for giving life. However, life could not have been the result of the Big Bang because life cannot come from non-life. Therefore, there must have been some kind of unique life that existed before the "Bang". So, what do we have before the creation of the universe? We have a unique type of energy as yet unexplained—a living, intelligent energy; one that cannot be created or destroyed—God.

"When a man sees God in all beings and all beings in God, and also God dwelling in his own Soul, how can he hate any living thing?"

— *Isa Upanishads*

Does the Soul Exist?

As long as there has been a debate concerning the existence of God there has been an equally on-going debate of whether or not humans have a soul—an immortal component that survives the death of the physical body. Are we a strictly physical creature or is there another part of us that we might call the spirit?

Once again, it is impossible to prove or disprove the existence of things that are incorporeal or non-physical. But is it reasonable to believe that a soul exists based on what we know and have observed in this life? Perhaps there is.

There has probably never been a philosopher who has not given an opinion on this subject. Descartes, Plato, Socrates, Pythagoras, Spinoza and Kant, to name a few all believed in the existence of a soul. But there were as many who disagreed, especially in more contemporary times. Each made their own determination using a variety of well-stated arguments. I will not share those theories at this time, given the volume and complexity of most. My argument is simple and straightforward, not as complicated and tedious as some, but I believe it is adequate to show that the existence of the soul as a separate entity from the body is a reasonable assumption.

As I have mentioned throughout this thesis, we live in a world of duality. This is obvious from several aspects. First of all, duality, in the sense of physical versus spiritual, is a matter of deductive reasoning based on our earlier assumptions.

1. God (non-physical) existed before matter (physical);
2. Physical (matter) came after the non-physical;
3. Therefore, being that they appeared separate in the beginning, they remain separate entities.

To understand the Spirit that is the Soul, we must have a better understanding of the Spirit that is God. But how can we understand something that is incomprehensible?

In his *Epistle 234*, St. Basil of Caesarea said,

> "...but we say that we know our God from His activities, but do not undertake to approach near to His essence. His activities come down to us, but His essence remains beyond our reach."

So, if we examine the activities of God we should be able to know something about God. For instance, in creating the universe, we can presume that God is all-powerful since a creator must be greater than its creation. So, it is all-powerful or omnipotent. We can also assume that since it is not limited by time or space, it is timeless, that is, it can be everywhere at once. So, it is omnipresent. And, finally, since it has always existed from the beginning, we must also assume that it will continue to exist so that it is immortal or eternal. Given that God is omnipresent, it exists in all things. Therefore, it is reasonable to assume that if God is eternal and God is in all things—humans included, then it would also be true that humans, having God in us, or being in God, we, too, would possess an eternal component. And since we acknowledge that our physical bodies are not eternal or immortal, having witnessed the decomposition of the physical form (body), we must assume that everything that has life, including humans, possess another element fashioned into the physical form (body) that represents the eternal component, or the "God part". We might call that part the Soul.

To further understand the reasonableness of the existence of the Soul we need to once again recognize and acknowledge the Universal Laws that exist in our world and impact the entire universe. You'll remember that one of these laws is the Law of Polarity (or the Law of Opposites or Contraries). This law states that for every quality and value there necessarily exists its opposite; but since both contrasting values are essential for making the other possible, we can conclude that together these opposites form a unique unity. With this understanding, and acknowledging that a human being is a single entity, and that it is also held to the Law of Polarity, we must conclude that we are a single form (body) constructed with two opposite parts: physical (tangible) and spiritual (intangible), mortal and immortal, body and Soul. Possessing these two components, humans satisfy the Universal Law of Polarity that applies to all earthly things.

In the book, *Mind Beyond Brain*, David E. Presti says it this way:

> "Within a strictly physicalist metaphysics—where there is a necessity that mind and consciousness be explained in terms of the properties of matter—this mind-body relationship may always be a problem. For there is a difference of category between the mental and the physical—consciousness is irreducibly subjective and experiential, and thus very different from physical stuff. That is precisely

what makes the mind-body problem hard—some would say impossible."[32]

He continues:

> "There is dual-aspect monism, where mind and matter are considered dual complementary aspects of an underlying neutral, beyond concept, reality."

In other words, there are two distinct aspects in human existence that function in tandem as a single unit.

Based on these arguments, it is reasonable to believe that humans, in fact, all living things are composed of an incorporeal element that we call a Soul. This is a reasonable conclusion.

In addition to the debate over the existence of the Soul, the concept of how the Soul functions as part of the human experience has also been the topic of discussion for centuries. However, if we continue using the analogy of the body and the Soul—one mirroring the other, we might make a reasonable comparison between the two. Briefly, our earthly form is constructed of two main components: the physical (body), consisting of skin, organs, bone and muscle; and the mental (brain), which acts as a sort of computer processor, receiving information from sensory neurons and then processing that information into action or reaction.

Contrarily, the Soul is where the personality and character of the individual is housed, and the Mind is where thought, memories, creativity, and unconsciousness reside. One part is the physical, or tangible (body and brain), the other, the spiritual, or

---

[32] David E. Presti. Mind Beyond Brain. Columbia University Press.

intangible (the Soul and the Mind): one part mortal, the other immortal.

But isn't the mind thought to be part of the brain? The difference is that one is physical and the other is non-physical. If consciousness is a result of brain activity, then when a person dies, consciousness will also be lost. And, if consciousness is lost, then life on the higher plane is also lost. Without consciousness we cannot evolve spiritually—we are dead and there is no metaphysical evolution—there is no immortality. Furthermore, God, being spirit (non-physical), and not possessing any physical components including a brain, would not be conscious and therefore, would not exist.

One source of evidence that consciousness lies beyond that of our normal functioning is provided by near death experiences. I mentioned this at the beginning of this book. In an article written January 16, 2019, Richard Martini interviewed Dr. Bruce Greyson, Professor of Psychiatric Medicine Carlson, Professor Emeritus of Psychiatry & Neurobehavioral Sciences, Former Director of Division of Perceptual Studies, Department of Psychiatry & Neurobehavioral Sciences University of Virginia Health System. This is what he had to say in regard to NDEs and consciousness.

> "We also have more sophisticated evidence from science of the link between the brain and consciousness; we can measure electricity in the brain during certain kinds of mental tasks, we can stimulate parts of the brain and record what experiences result and we can remove parts of the brain and observe the effects on behavior.
>
> "All this evidence suggests the brain is indeed involved in thinking, perception and memory,

but it doesn't necessary suggest the brain *causes* those thoughts or memories... all the studies showing brain areas associated with different mental functions only show correlation, not causation.

"Thoughts, perception and memories could take place in a consciousness somewhere separate from the brain, but are then received and processed by the brain. Much like a phone, radio or TV; the signal, the message is created somewhere else, but your cell phone is necessary to receive and process the message."

In addition to NDEs, past life experiences also provide evidence of reincarnation. Past life experiences are very different phenomena than near death experiences. As I have mentioned previously, I am skeptical of testimonials from adults who tell tales about memories of a past life because the brain is complex and has the potential of playing tricks on us in various ways— fabricating memories where there were none or associating images that we have seen or stories that we have heard with our own memories or experiences. However, when it comes to young children who have not lived long enough to have had many experiences or been exposed to other external impressions, these testimonials are much more credible.

Ian Stevenson[33] largely created a new area of scientific research when he began studying cases of children who reported memories of previous lives. In 1975,

---

[33] Ian Stevenson was the chair of the Department of Psychiatry at the University of Virginia in 1957. His research led him to continue to investigate the phenomenon for the next forty years.

Stevenson published a four-volume series called *Cases of the Reincarnation Type.*

After reading a paper that Stevenson had written, the Journal of the American Medical Association wrote:

> "In regard to reincarnation he has painstakingly and unemotionally collected a detailed series of cases from India, cases in which the evidence is difficult to explain on any other grounds."[34]

So many of these investigations involving children and their past life memories are fascinating. I will share only one brief example of the kind of memories these children share.

Jim Tucker, a psychiatry professor at the University of Virginia and the author of the book, *Return to Life: Extraordinary Cases of Children Who Remember Past Lives,* has been involved for many years in the study of children who experience past life memories. He also served as the medical director of the University's Child and Family Psychiatry Clinic.

The following is from an article written by Michael Jawer that appeared in Psychology Today, December 13, 2014.

> "When Ryan was 4, he began directing imaginary movies. Shouts of 'Action!' often echoed from his room. But the play became a concern for Ryan's parents when he began waking up in the middle of the night screaming and clutching his chest, saying he dreamed his heart exploded when he was in Hollywood.

---

[34] Quote copied from Mind Beyond Brain. Presti.

> "His mother asked his doctor about the episodes. Night terrors, the doctor said. He'll outgrow them. Then one night, as his mother tucked Ryan into bed, Ryan suddenly took hold of her hand. 'Mama,' he said. 'I think I used to be someone else.'
>
> "He said he remembered a big white house and a swimming pool. It was in Hollywood, many miles from his Oklahoma home. He said he had three sons, but that he couldn't remember their names. He began to cry, asking his mother over and over why he couldn't remember their names."

The article continues to explain that his mother was confused and was experiencing a sort of shock. Ryan was insistent on the fact that he remembered these things. Concerned for her son, his mother started researching reincarnation. She went so far as to obtain books on Hollywood's history from the library.

> "One day, as Ryan and his mom paged through one of the Hollywood books, Ryan stopped at a black-and-white still taken from a 1930s movie, *Night After Night*. Two men in the center of the picture were confronting one another. Four other men surrounded them. His mother didn't recognize any of the faces, but Ryan pointed to one of the men in the middle. 'Hey Mama,' he said. 'That's George. We did a picture together.' His finger then shot over to a man on the right, wearing an overcoat and a scowl. 'That guy's me. I found me!'

His mother was able to confirm that the man who Ryan called George in the photo was indeed George, George

Raft, a film star from the 1930s and 1940s. However, she was not able to identify the man who Ryan claimed was him. She found Jim Tucker's name on the internet and contacted him with Ryan's story. After some research by a film archivist, they found that the man who Ryan claimed to be was Martin Martyn, an extra in the film.

> "Not long afterward, Tucker and the family traveled to California to meet Martyn's daughter, who'd been tracked down by researchers working with Tucker on a documentary. Tucker sat down with the woman before her meeting with Ryan. She'd been reluctant to help, but during her talk with Tucker, she confirmed dozens of facts Ryan had given about her father.
>
> "Ryan said he danced in New York. Martyn was a Broadway dancer. Ryan said he was also an 'agent,' and that people where he worked had changed their names. Martyn worked for years at a well-known talent agency in Hollywood—where stage names are often created—after his dancing career ended. Ryan said his old address had 'Rock' in its name. Martyn lived at 825 North Roxbury Drive in Beverly Hills. Ryan said he knew a man named Senator Five. Martyn's daughter said she had a picture of her father with a Senator Ives, Irving Ives, of New York, who served in the U.S. Senate from 1947 to 1959. And yes, Martin Martyn had three sons. The daughter, of course, knew their names."

This story and the fact that so many of Ryan's claims were substantiated is difficult to repudiate. For nearly 15 years, Tucker has been investigating claims made by children, usually between the ages of 2 and 6 years old, who claim to have had past lives. The children are sometimes able to provide enough detail about those lives that their stories can be traced back to an actual person—rarely famous and often entirely unknown to the family—who died years before. Certainly, there are those cases that don't prove to be credible. But Tucker says that in cases like Ryan's:

> "The most logical, scientific explanation for a claim is as simple as it is astounding: Somehow, the child recalls memories from another life."

Additionally, he says that nearly 20 percent of the children studied have scar-like birthmarks or even unusual deformities that closely match marks or injuries the person whose life the child recalls received at or near his or her death.

These memories and claims generally disappear around the age of 6.

> "It's conceivable that in some way consciousness could be expressed in a new life," Tucker says.

Tucker has documented over 2500 credible child testimonials from countries around the world.

The evidence for reincarnation is significant—evidence provided by universal laws, creation, near death experiences and past life experiences. When the brain dies, life goes on.

But, we might ask, if the mind houses our thoughts and consciousness, what about diseases like Alzheimers? Doesn't that disease affect the mind? Let's return to our earlier example. Our brain (physical) represents a computer processor. It receives signals and other information that it files away or processes and responds to. Our mind (non-physical), then, represents the computer user. As long as the computer is working correctly, the user can access and use the information provided by the processor. But once the processor stops working correctly, the information, while still present, is no longer accessible. It is the physical component that malfunctions and not the non-physical. In essence, the brain is the *bridge* between the physical and the non-physical.

"Children (the ignorant) pursue external pleasures; (thus) they fall into the wide-spread snare of death. But the wise, knowing the nature of immortality, do not seek the permanent among fleeting things."

— *The Upanishads*

Reincarnation and God

The doctrine of Reincarnation teaches that God is beyond our comprehension. We have discussed this earlier in the discourse. We can only know about God through God's activities in the world. But even then, our understanding is inadequate in grasping what and who God really is.

There seems to have always been an inclination by humans throughout the ages to humanize God while deifying humans. Xenophanes, a Greek theologian and philosopher who lived around 500 BCE said:

> "In my opinion mortals have created their gods with the dress and voice and appearance of mortals. If cattle and horses, or lions, had hands, or were able to draw with their feet and produce the works which men do, horses would draw the forms of gods like horses, and cattle like cattle, and they would make the gods' bodies the same shape as their own. The Ethiopians say that their gods have snub noses and black skins, while the Thracians say that theirs have blue eyes and red hair."

But how can we relate to a God who seems to be unreachable? Throughout the ages it has been taught that God is like a father or a good friend. But to think of God as being in such an earthly relationship is to limit how we should envision this magnificent, indescribable Being. Our relationship with the Creator is beyond that of what we define as a friendship or even that of a parent.

The Kena Upanishad says it like this:

> "Him our eyes cannot see, nor words express;
> He cannot be grasped even by the mind.
> We do not know, we cannot understand,
> Because He is different from the known
> And He is different from the unknown."[35]

So, is God a personal God or is God distant and unreachable? According to the doctrine of rebirth the answer is—yes and no. The answer can be found in attempting to grasp *what* God is. R.W. Trine explains it this way:

> "The great central fact of the universe is that spirit of infinite life and power that is back of all, that manifests itself in and through all. This spirit of infinite life and power that is back of all is what I call God. I care not what term you may use, be it Kindly Light, Providence, the Over-Soul, Omnipotence, or whatever term may be most convenient, so long as we are agreed in regard to the great central fact itself. God then fills the universe alone, so that all is from Him and in Him, and there is nothing that is outside. He is the life of our life, our very life itself. We are partakers of the life of God; and though we differ from Him in that we are individualized spirits, while He is the Infinite Spirit, including us, as well as all else besides, yet in essence the life of God and the life of man are identically the same, and so are one. They differ not in essence or quality; they differ in degree."[36]

---

[35] The Kena Upanishad. Vs.3-4.

[36] R. W. Trine: *In Tune with the Infinite*, 26th thousand, N. Y., 1899.

God is universal *life*. Friends may come and go and relatives might fail us, but God is always present. We can see an example of that in the consistency of our universal laws that are always dependable and trustworthy to be the same aeon after aeon. God's sustaining power is universal.

However, God *is* also actively involved in our individual lives. When we realize that God is everywhere—in every living thing, then we will understand that God is present in a friend or in a relative, or even in a stranger who seems to appear at just the right time—in our time of need, to offer us the help we require.

There is an old story that illustrates this fact. I have heard it told many different ways so I will tell as I remember it, taking some literary license. There was a great flood following a terrible storm. A man crawled up on his roof to escape the rising waters. He was trapped. Before long a boat approached the man and the people in the boat asked the man if he needed help. The man replied that he did not because God was going to save him. As the water rose and the man became more fearful, another boat happened by. Once again the people in the boat asked the man if he needed help. Once again the man replied that he did not because God would save him. Finally, the water had risen so that the man had to climb onto his chimney to avoid being swept away by the flood. This time, a helicopter hovered overhead and the pilot yelled to the man to grab hold of the rope he was lowering. The man yelled back that he did not need the rope. God would save him. Unfortunately, the man was finally swept away by the waters and drowned. When the man approached God in the afterlife and asked God why he didn't perform a miracle and save him. God replied that he did. He had sent the man two boats and a helicopter.

We are someone's miracle. All of creation is an example of God's miraculous works. God is in all things, and God makes use of all creation to perform His miracles. God is whatever we need when we need it. God is the air we breathe, the water we drink and the sun that gives us warmth. God is the child that we hold, the friend that we love and the enemy that we despise.

One of my favorite spiritual verses is from the Gnostic Gospels, the Secret Book of John. This is the way the writer describes God:

> "...The One is a sovereign that has nothing over it. It is God and Parent, Father of the All, the invisible one that is over the All, that is incorruptible, that is pure light at which no eye can gaze.
>
> The One is illimitable, since there
>   is nothing before it to limit it,
> unfathomable, since there is nothing
>   before it to fathom it,
> immeasurable, since there was nothing
>   before it to measure it,
> invisible, since nothing has seen it,
> eternal, since it exists eternally,
> unutterable, since nothing could
>   comprehend it to utter it,
> unnamable, since there is nothing
>   before it to give it a name.
>
> The One is immeasurable light, pure, holy, immaculate. It is unutterable, and is perfect in incorruptibility. Not that it is just perfection, or blessedness, or divinity: it is much greater.

The One is not corporeal and it not incorporeal.
The One is not large and it is not small.
It is impossible to say,
> How much is it?
> What kind is it?
> For no one can understand it.

The One is not among the things that exist, but it is much greater. Not that it is greater. Rather, as it is in itself, it is not a part of the aeons of time. For whatever is part of a realm was once prepared by another. Time was not allotted to it, since it receives nothing from anyone; what would be received would be on loan. The one who is first does not need to receive anything from another. It beholds itself in its light.

> The One is majestic and has an immeasurable purity.
> The One is a realm that gives a realm,
> life that gives life,
> a blessed one that gives blessedness,
> knowledge that gives knowledge,
> a good one that gives goodness,
> mercy that gives mercy and redemption,
> grace that gives grace.

Not that the One possesses this. Rather, the One gives immeasurable and incomprehensible light.

What shall I tell you about it? Its eternal realm is incorruptible, at peace, dwelling in silence, at rest, before everything. It is the head of all realms, and it is the one who sustains them through its goodness."[37]

---

[37] The Nag Hammadi Scriptures: The Secret Book of John, Edited by

The truth is that in a universe vast and unknown where there are millions of galaxies and billions of planets, we are infinitesimal organisms. We might dominate the animal kingdom on this planet but when it comes to the universe, we are non-essential creatures. God does not need our praise or worship, our love or our devotion. God does not need our prayers or even our acknowledgement. If God needed any of these things, it would render God dependent on us in some way. If this is true then God is something less than perfect because dependence would render it imperfect. On the contrary, we offer praise because that's the right thing for us to do out of adoration and respect for the Creator.

God is Creator, Provider and Sustainer. As the Creator, God has fashioned a universe that functions efficiently and consistently. Through a perfectly designed creation, the universe and everything in it is moving precisely as planned in order to reach its intended destination; a destination that is a mystery to us.

God is the Provider in that God has given us everything that we need to survive and to successfully achieve our own personal destination, that of perfection and reunion with the Source of life.

As Sustainer, God is the Vitality and Energy of life in all things.

Marvin Meyer, (HarperOne, New York, 2007), 108-09.

One Life

A basic principle of Reincarnation is that there is one life in the universe. Only one life actually exists—one. This one and only life is the First Cause of all things. But this original life is not defined in the same way as we define physical life on earth. This one life has no need to grow or reproduce. It is totally self-sufficient. It doesn't depend on anyone or anything for its existence or to enhance its existence.

To better understand the concept of "one life", we should review what we have already discussed in a previous chapter.

We have shown that the First Cause was a living entity. And since this First Life has always existed and was not created, we must assume that life is not and cannot be created, but that it can only come from another life; and, since this unique First Life had no beginning there is no reason to believe that it will have an end since both beginning and ending are a value of time and something that has always existed is timeless. So, this one Life is eternal—immortal. It had no beginning and will have no end.

Through observation and experience, we know that when life comes from another life, it partakes of the life of its procreator, that is, it is not a new life created from nothing, but rather it shares this new life from a life that already exists. We know this because we observe the process of procreation in humans and other creatures and organisms where eggs are fertilized by living sperm. Furthermore, the new life shares in many of the attributes of the parents. In the physical world, the new life shares the physical form of its parents and many of their attributes. Likewise, in the spiritual dimension, the

First Life shared its immortal life with a newly formed organism. It became the first physical manifestation of the First Life. Since the life that was shared by the First Life was immortal, that immortality became an attribute of the newly formed organism. Therefore, all living things that exist are merely manifestations of the First Life in different forms, existing in various degrees of that Life, but all sharing the attribute of immortality. Some call that "First Life", God, and the life that was shared, the Soul or Spirit.

Science tells us that energy cannot be created. Therefore, all forms of energy that we witness throughout the universe is simply energy. It is not new energy or old energy it is energy. Similarly, all life that we witness in the universe is not new or old life, but simply life. Life that has always been and will always be.

Does that mean that all living things contain God? Yes. God is omnipresent, and being so, exists in some degree in all living things. Does that imply that all living things have a soul? No. The soul is only present in those living things that have reached the stage of spiritual development and have achieved consciousness.[38]

---

[38] Here, of course, we are faced with an ongoing debate: do animals like dogs and cats and monkeys reincarnate? All living things possess in some degree the one life that is shared by God. That life, regardless of what form it is in at any time experiences spiritual evolution just as the earliest forms of history have experienced physical evolution. With each reincarnation, the life moves forward through the hierarchy of forms until it reaches the stage of a form that also possesses consciousness (Soul). Therefore, animals, being in an advanced stage of spiritual development, although not yet to the stage of consciousness, are destined to eventually reach that stage of residing in a conscious life form. However, a soul only resides in a conscious life form. God breathed His breath of conscious life (soul) only into man (humans).

Given that God is omnipresent, God is in all living things and yet God is beyond all things. There is no life that exists that has not always existed in some degree and in some form from the very beginning because God has always existed and in God all life has its existence. From the very beginning, all things have been, as God has been.

Because God is present in all living things there is no need for additional lives. This one life is sufficient. Any other life would be unnecessary. Just as all things have always existed in various forms, we too, have always existed. Our personality and character have been dormant like seeds waiting for the opportunity to grow. We are nothing more than manifestations of the one life but in a lesser degree, having been purposefully planted in a physical environment as part of the physical universe.

> "Thus do men imagine themselves separate from one another, when all the time their soul is nothing more than a drop of the divine Ocean, hidden momentarily in a perishable body."[39]

In the Vedas, the earliest known spiritual writings, the emphasis throughout the text is on the assumption that God exists in all of creation—that God permeates the universe. When the writers speak of God they use a proper name but when they refer to God dwelling inside of an individual they refer to God as Self. That's because it is the combination of one's personality and character blended with the indwelling of God that creates a person's true Self.

---

[39] Théophile Pascal. *Reincarnation: A Study in Human Evolution.*

Self is in all of us and Jesus certainly believed this when he said:

> "...that all of them may be one, Father, just as you are in me and I am in you. May they also be in us so that the world may believe that you have sent me. I have given them the glory that you gave me, that they may be one as we are one..."[40]

And,

> "I and the Father are one."[41]

In the Upanishads, a son is asking his father for answers to life's biggest questions. Concerning God, or Self, his father says,

> "It is everywhere, though we see it not.
> Just so, dear one, the Self is everywhere,
> Within all things, although we see him not.
> There is nothing that does not come from him.
> Of everything he is the inmost Self.
> He is truth; he is the Self-supreme.
> You are that, Shvetaketu, you are that."[42]

Al-Hallaj, a student of the 10th century Islamic mystic al-Junayd wrote this poem of God:

> "I am He whom I love, and He whom I love is I;
> We are two spirits dwelling in one body.
> If thou seest me, thou seest Him,
> And if thou seest Him, thou seest us both."[43]

---

[40] Bible, John 17:20-22.
[41] Bible, John 10:30.
[42] *The Changogya Upanishad* ,Chapter VI, 13:3.
[43] Quoted in Nicholson, *The Mystics of Islam*, Routledge, Kegan Paul, London, 1914, p. 151

Another bit of Biblical endorsement is from the writer of the Book of Genesis. In Genesis 2:7 he writes:

> "Then the Lord God formed a man from the dust of the ground and breathed into his nostrils the breath of life, and the man became a living being."[44]

God "formed" man and then He *breathed* into his nostrils the "breath of life". Whose life was the breath from? God. God didn't create a new life, God breathed his *own* breath, the life-giving breath, into man. They shared the same breath and the *same* life.

One Reality

To further understand the idea of "one life" it is necessary to understand that there is only one reality and that reality is God. Nothing exists outside of this entity. Unarguably, for us, at this time and in this environment, we recognize this physical world as our present reality. But our reality, as we experience it now with its duality (physical and spiritual), is merely a transient reality within the absolute reality that is God.

This life is only an illusion of what is real. Like the inhabitants of Plato's allegory of the "cave"[45] our

---

[44] Genesis 2:7
[45] The example of the cave comes from Plato's *Republic*. In brief, to make a point regarding Forms, Socrates shares an allegory about a group of prisoners who have been isolated in a cave all of their lives. They have been chained so that they cannot move or turn their heads. In front of them is a wall where they can see the shadow of objects that are being produced by puppeteers from behind them who are using real objects to produce the shadows. As the prisoners discuss what they are seeing on the wall, they consider the shadows as real objects rather than shadows. This is their reality. Even when one of the prisoners escapes and has the opportunity to see what is real and returns to the cave and tries to convince the others that what they are seeing are not real forms but only shadows, they threaten to kill him if he persists in insisting that what they are seeing is not reality.

present condition is all that we know and therefore we assume that it must be all that exists. But just as the eyes of the inhabitants of Plato's cave were blinded by their environment, so ours are blinded by our present condition.

Why Aren't We Perfect?

But if our life is one and the same as that of the Creator, and the Creator is perfect and all-knowing and all-powerful, and we share that life then why don't we also share in these attributes? Why aren't we spiritually perfect?

> "Indeed and in truth, then, in Him we live and move and have our being. He is the life of our life, our very life itself. We have received, we are continually receiving our life from Him. We are partakers of the life of God; and though we differ from Him in that we are individualized spirits, while He is the Infinite Spirit including us as well as all else beside, yet in essence the life of God and the life of man are identically the same, and so are one. They differ not in essence, in quality; they differ in degree."[46]

Our spirits differ in *degree*. Previously, we explained how we are composed of two distinct components, very different and yet integrated into one single physical form. Remember what Socrates observed. The two components that constitute our existence here on earth are opposites: physical and non-physical (spiritual). When one value affects or takes dominance over the

---

[46] Ralph Waldo Trine. *In Tune with the Infinite; or, Fullness of Peace, Power, and Plenty*

other, the result is that the value of the one being affected is altered.

On this plane, we are physical forms. This world is 100% materialistic. Because we are subjected to the limitations of physical existence like that of time and space, and we grow from infancy surrounded by tangible things, it is reasonable that we should lose sight of who we really are. We become part of the physical world that we see and experience around us. On the scale of materialism versus spiritualism, we move away from the non-physical and closer to the pole of the physical.

In fact, the influence of the material world is so powerful, that we become virtually 100% human even though our spiritual life is still very much intact. It is not until we reach the age of consciousness, the age of decision-making, that we have the capacity to begin to move the needle on the scale away from the physical and closer to the spiritual through our decision-making capability. Our daily goal is not to be perfect. It is to become more perfect.

Let's take a minute and confront a question that is looming in many minds at this point: why did God choose to share life with physical forms in the first place? It has been my objective to only offer information that is supported by reason and evidence. Unfortunately, there can be no reasonable explanation to this question because who can know the mind of God? Who can surmise why the Creator chose to create the universe as it exists today? Perhaps it exists for the reason the Psalmist has said:

> The heavens declare the glory of God;
>   the skies proclaim the work of his hands.
> ² Day after day they pour forth speech;
>   night after night they reveal knowledge.
> ³ They have no speech, they use no words;
>   no sound is heard from them.
> ⁴ Yet their voice goes out into all the earth,
>   their words to the ends of the world.[47]

Maybe that's why we humans have evolved to this higher level of consciousness and intellect. Perhaps, we, too, are here to demonstrate the works of God, showing through our deeds the goodness of the Creator.

---

[47] Psalms 19:1-4

"But the fruit of the Spirit is love, joy, peace, forbearance, kindness, goodness, faithfulness, gentleness and self-control. Against such things there is no law."

— Galatians 5:22-23

Reincarnation and Physical Existence

So, here we are: physical creatures in a physical world—not wholly physical, but constructed miraculously with two unifying but opposing components, physical and spiritual, that provide us with the opportunity to experience a unique journey in the quest for perfection.

We've already shown how Reincarnation complies with our earthly reality and the Laws of the Universe. Now let me attempt to explain how Reincarnation makes sense when applied to life on earth. Earlier in this discourse I brought up the three big questions: where did we come from, why are we here (our purpose, meaning of life), and where are we going? Coming from a Christian background, I often wondered why it was constantly stressed that we should strive to develop a virtuous character. In the New Testament, Galatians 5:22-23 the writer lists the fruits of the Spirit:

> "But the fruit of the Spirit is love, joy, peace, forbearance, kindness, goodness, faithfulness, gentleness and self-control. Against such things there is no law."

But why should we endeavor to become patient or kind or compassionate or loving? As mentioned previously, according to most religious ideologies, when all is said and done, we all die and everything we've accomplished, including our character dies with us. According to Christianity and Islam, those who die but have believed in certain things like Jesus being the Son of God or Mohammad being the prophet of Allah, will experience eternal bliss—heaven or Paradise.

However, this Heaven or Paradise has nothing at all to do with our life on earth other than making those important theological decisions that determine our fate. In this new after-life, utopian existence, our efforts to cultivate a virtuous character in this life are meaningless. Once we enter Paradise, we are destined to do nothing for the rest of eternity other than sing praises, worship and enjoy streets of gold and luxurious mansions. (Which, by the way, are materialistic values that we are taught to disdain on earth but value in heaven). But, there doesn't seem to be any place for utilizing a virtuous character. So why improve as humans? Why work to attain the fruits of the Spirit? According to Christian doctrine, once a person has gone through the ritual of salvation they no longer need to worry about the future. They have heaven "in the bag" so to speak. So where is the motivation? What reason can there be for becoming a better person? As I stated previously, patience, compassion and all of the other virtues might be of value in this life, but they have no relevance in heaven. There is no incentive for improvement.

Additionally, the Christian doctrine teaches that God lowered itself to become human. Therefore, humans have no need to attempt to raise themselves to God. Perfection is a gift that requires no effort on our part.

Reincarnation addresses these issues much differently. Reincarnation teaches that the Soul is on a continuous journey, traveling from life to life with each life building on the previous one. As a result, the virtuous character traits that were developed in one life are maintained in each subsequent life until, at last, the Soul reaches the goal of perfection—becoming one with the Creator. So, there is a reason for developing these valuable traits, now and in the future.

I would like to take a minute and briefly offer a side note. I would like to address the difference between reincarnation and resurrection. With reincarnation the Soul takes on a new physical form or body. In the concept of resurrection, it is taught that the physical body that dies is given new life. Once again, I will refer to nature as our textbook. The only possible indication of a resurrection of this type was envisioned by very primitive humans who observed the sun rising and setting and considered it the death and resurrection of a new day (new sun). However, we now know that that concept is erroneous. The idea of giving new life to a dead and decayed body simply has no evidence or foundation except through legends and religious fables.

In contrast, we have many examples of rebirth. We can use the simple analogy of a plant. The dying plant crumbles and decays. However, the seed, lying dormant in the soil slowly emerges as a new plant. Within that tiny seed are stored all of the characteristics that will be manifested in the new plant as it grows to maturity. Certainly, the soil in which it is planted (the environment) can impact its development in some small way, but the characteristics of the plant have already been established through hundreds of years of evolutionary formation. So it is with the germ or seed of human life. The non-physical characteristics and personality of the developing Soul have already been formed through hundreds of years of past-life evolution. We are who we have become through past lives.

"It is more especially after death that the soul, set free from its illusory sheaths, makes an impartial review of its recent incarnation, attentively following its actions and their consequences, noting its errors and failures, along with their motives and causes. In this school it grows in knowledge and power;..."

— William Walker Atkinson

Reincarnation and the After Life

As we discussed earlier, our Spirit consists of two parts: the Mind and the Soul. Together, these two components constitute who we are. At death, the physical body falls away, as do all of the other physical aspects that were part of life on earth. However, our essence—who we really are—our personality, our character, our talents, our preferences and other intangible values remain with us locked in our Spirit. Again, those are the things that make us who we are, who we have become over the ages, through past lives. The Soul evolves as we travel from life to life, making decisions that shape and mold us along the journey. There are many speculations concerning what occurs to the Soul after we die. I will offer what is considered by many Reincarnationists to be the most popular theory and then explain why it is the most reasonable.

The most popular and tenable idea supported by the most reasonableness is that when a person dies and leaves the physical body behind, they enter into a dimension of peace where the Soul/Mind (Spirit) can rest from the stress and experiences of life on earth. Just as it is on earth where a day ends with a time of rest, so also in the afterlife, the Soul, having completed a life cycle is allowed time to rejuvenate.

It is reasonable to assume that this place of rest is in a dimension far different than that of earth. So there is, of course, no measure of time since our time values are unique and would not be the same in any other environment.

Then, for a period, the Spirit is allowed to review the decisions and experiences of life on earth. During this time, the Soul is given an opportunity to understand how each decision impacted others, and altered the course of their own journey. These memories will become important lessons in the quest for improvement.

> "Others held that there was a period of waiting and rest between incarnations, in which the soul 'mentally digested' the experiences of the last life just completed, and then considered and meditated over the mistakes it had made, and determined to rectify the mistakes in the next life—it being held that when the soul was relieved of the necessities of material existence, it could think more clearly of the moral nature of its acts, and would be able to realize the spiritual side of itself more distinctly, in addition to having the benefit of the spiritual perspective occasioned by its distance from the active scenes of life, and thus being able to better gauge the respective "worth-whileness" of the things of material life."[48]

Then, at some point afterwards, when the Soul is ready for rebirth, all memories are erased. Nothing is remembered. Why aren't memories retained? The reasons are quite simple. Memories that have accumulated over several lifetimes, both good and bad, would continuously flood the mind. Pleasant memories might cause an individual to live in the past. Unpleasant memories might cause depression or guilt that would destroy the optimism needed to successfully move forward in the new life. Actually, when carefully

---

[48] William Walker Atkinson.

considered, memories are of little use. It is what we learn from our experiences that is important.

> "Let the reader lay down this book, and then endeavor to remember what happened in his twelfth year. He will not remember more than one or two, or a half dozen, events in that year—perhaps not one, in the absence of a diary, or perhaps even with the aid of one. The majority of the happenings of the three hundred and sixty-five days of that year are as a blank—as if they never had happened, so far as the memory is concerned. And yet, the same "I," or Ego, persists, and the person's character has certainly been affected and influenced by the experiences and lessons of that year. Perhaps in that year, the person may have acquired certain knowledge that he uses in his everyday life. And so, in this case, as with Reincarnation, the "essence" of the experiences is preserved, while the details are forgotten. For that is the Reincarnationist contention. As a matter of fact, advanced occultists, and other Reincarnationists, claim that nothing is really forgotten, but that every event is stored away in some of the recesses of the mind, below the level of consciousness-which idea agrees with that of modern psychologists."[49]

So, while the actual memories disappear in subsequent lives, the valuable lessons that were learned from those experiences are retained, locked away in the unconscious. Then, in a future life when a similar situation is encountered, or a decision that has been

---
[49] William Walker Atkinson.

faced in a past life occurs, what was learned from that past experience and retained in the unconscious, surfaces as intuition. It becomes the proverbial "angel on our shoulder" guiding us to make the correct decision. We still have the option to decide otherwise, but these intuitions are usually accurate in their guidance. An article was published on the Psychological Science website concerning intuition:

> "Many people use the phrase 'intuition' to describe a sensation or feeling they have when making decisions, but these are only descriptions, they don't provide strong evidence that we can use unconscious information in our brain or body to guide our behavior. This is the first time we have been able to show strong evidence that something like intuition does actually exist.
>
> "To measure intuition, the researchers designed an experiment in which participants were exposed to emotional images outside conscious awareness as they attempted to make accurate decisions. The results of the study demonstrate that even when people were unaware of the images, they were still able to use information from the images to make more confident and accurate decisions.
>
> "These data suggest that we can use unconscious information in our body or brain to help guide us through life, to enable better decisions, faster decisions, and be more confident in the decisions we make."[50]

---

[50] Psychological Science. Volume 27, Issue 5. Pages 622-634. *Measuring Intuition: Nonconscious Emotional Information Boosts Decision Accuracy*

Psychologist William James makes this statement concerning a "deeper" consciousness:

> "I cannot but think that the most important step forward that has occurred in psychology since I have been a student of that science is the discovery, first made in 1886, that, in certain subjects at least, there is not only the consciousness of the ordinary field, with its usual centre and margin, but an addition thereto in the shape of a set of memories, thoughts, and feelings which are extra-marginal and outside of the primary consciousness altogether, but yet must be classed as conscious facts of some sort, able to reveal their presence by unmistakable signs. I call this the most important step forward because, unlike the other advances which psychology has made, this discovery has revealed to us an entirely unsuspected peculiarity in the constitution of human nature. No other step forward which psychology has made can proffer any such claim as this.
>
> "The impulses may take the direction of automatic speech or writing, the meaning of which the subject himself may not understand even while he utters it; and generalizing this phenomenon, Mr. Myers has given the name of automatism, sensory or motor, emotional or intellectual, to this whole sphere of effects, due to "uprushes" into the ordinary consciousness of energies originating in the subliminal parts of the mind."[51]

and Confidence. Galang Lufityanto, Chris Donkin, Joel Pearson

In an article that appeared in Psychology Today, December 13, 2014, Jim Tucker, a psychiatry professor at the University of Virginia who has conducted an extensive study on past-life memories said:

> "How exactly the consciousness, or at least memories, of one person might transfer to another is obviously a mystery, but the answers might be found within the foundations of quantum physics. Scientists have long known that matter like electrons and protons produces events only when observed. A simplified example: Take light and shine it through a screen with two slits cut in it. Behind the screen, put a photographic plate that records the light. When the light is unobserved as it travels, the plate shows it went through both slits. But what happens when the light is observed? The plate shows the particles go through just one of the slits. The light's behavior changes, and the only difference is that it is being observed. There's plenty of debate on what that might mean. But Tucker, like Max Planck, the father of quantum physics, believes that discovery shows that the physical world is affected by, and even derived from the non-physical, from consciousness. If that's true, then consciousness doesn't require a three-pound brain to exist, Tucker says, and so there's no reason to think that consciousness would end with it. It's conceivable that in some way consciousness could be expressed in a new life…"

---

[51] James. *The Varieties of Religious Experience: A Study in Human Nature*

Science still has no answer as to where instinct and intuition come from. However, the idea that these influences come from experiences from past lives makes sense. The more we are sensitive to the guidance of this inner voice, the more active it becomes.

> "It is more especially after death that the soul, set free from its illusory sheaths, makes an impartial review of its recent incarnation, attentively following its actions and their consequences, noting its errors and failures, along with their motives and causes. In this school it grows in knowledge and power; and when, in a future incarnation, the same difficulties present themselves anew, it is better equipped for the struggle; what has been learned, is retained within the soul; it knows, where formerly it was ignorant, and by the "voice of conscience," tells the personality what its duty is."[52]

Before rebirth, the individual's Soul seeks parents that will provide what is best and required to take the Soul to the next level of development. This is accomplished by way of another universal law, the Law of Attraction. Simply put, the law states that objects, thoughts, ideas and people are attracted and drawn to others of similar value. "Birds of a feather flock together" sort of thing. There is some scientific application of this law but I will not venture there in this discussion. This "Law" has been used and misused by many but I will simply refer to observation as evidence that this concept is valid.

---

[52] Théophile Pascal.

As mentioned, the Soul searches for the best parents in the best environment to help it in its spiritual evolutionary development. However, what is best is not always what is comfortable. Sometimes the new environment is filled with conflict if conflict is what is needed to help the Soul build a more virtuous character and advance toward the goal.

The Soul, where the personality and character lives, and the Mind that houses intelligence and wisdom and talents, then travels with the Soul being reincarnated and resides with the child being born. So, all of the talents developed, skills refined, interests pursued and character cultivated in past lives continues to exist in the reincarnated individual. Each life is a new leg of the pilgrimage, providing new opportunities for growth and development in the journey to perfection.

"Nobody can imagine the amount of latent power which a minute germ of life possesses until it expresses in gross form on the physical plane. By seeing the seed of a Banyan tree, one who has never seen the tree cannot imagine what powers lie dormant in it."

— *Swami Abhedananda*

Reincarnation and Heredity

The true seed of existence resides within the spiritual being. That seed carries with it the personality, character attributes, interests, talents and lessons learned from past lives. But if all of these qualities are already present in some form, then what role does heredity play? In the spiritual areas of development heredity has little influence.

> "It is a part of this argument to assume that if all souls were freshly created, by the same Creator, and from the same material, they would resemble each other very closely, and in fact would be practically identical. And, it is urged, the fact that every child is different in tastes, temperament, qualities, nature, etc., independent of heredity and environment, then it must follow that the difference must be sought for further back. Children of the same parents differ very materially in nature, disposition, etc.; in fact, strangers are often more alike than children of the same parents, born within a few years of each other, and reared in the same environment. Those having much experience with young babies know that course. The infant a few hours born shows a gentleness, or a lack of it—a yielding or a struggle, a disposition to adjust itself, or a stubbornness, etc. And as the child grows, these traits show more plainly, and the nature of the individual asserts itself, subject, of course, to a moulding and shaping, but always asserting its original character in some way. Not only in the matter of disposition but in the

matter of tastes, tendencies, moral inclinations, etc., do the children differ...And it will be noticed that in the studies to which the child is attracted, it seems to learn almost without effort, as if it were merely re-learning some favorite study, momentarily forgotten. And in the case of the disliked study, every step is attended with toil. In some cases the child seems to learn every branch with the minimum effort, and with practically no effort; while in other cases the child has to plod wearily over every branch, as if breaking entirely new ground. And this continues into after life (adulthood), when the adult finds this thing or that thing into which he naturally fits as if it were made for him, the knowledge concerning it coming to him like the lesson of yesterday.

"Heredity does not seem to account for it—nor does environment answer the requirements. Some other factor is there—is it Reincarnation?"[53]

Another curious phenomenon concerns childhood and youthful genius. Consider this greatly abbreviated list of examples:

Blaise Pascal – (Mathematics, physics) wrote a treatise on vibrating bodies at the age of nine.

Lev Landau – (Mathematics) Mastered calculus at age 13.

William Cullen Bryant – (Poet) published his first poem at age 10 and his first book of political satire poems at age 13.

---

[53] William Walker Atkinson. (Kindle Locations 1368-1395).

Emily Bear – (Music) Composed and released her first piano album at age five.

Wolfgang Amadeus Mozart – (Music) - His first compositions were Andante (K. 1a) and Allegro at age 4.

And, that is just a minute sampling of the total number of children who have exhibited special talents and abilities.

> "Allied to this phenomenon is that of "youthful genius"—in fact, genius of any age, for that matter, for genius itself seems to be out of the category of the ordinary cause of heredity and environment, and to have its roots in some deeper, richer soil.
>
> "In many cases these children are born of parents and grandparents deficient in the particular branches of knowledge evidenced by the child. Babes scarcely able to sit on the piano stool, or to hold the violin, have begun to play in a way that certainly indicated previous knowledge and technique, often composing original productions in an amazing manner."[54]

Swami Abhedananda adds:

> "Does heredity explain such cases? No. These illustrations are sufficient to disprove the theory of "cumulative heredity". "Cumulative" means gradual-ness. The believers in this theory say that a genius is the result of cumulative heredity, that is, it presents itself by degrees from less genius to greater and still greater and so on. In

---
[54] ibid., (Kindle Locations 1396-1402).

> the whole history of the genealogy of geniuses, like Homer, Plato, Shakespeare, Goethe, Raphael, there never was in their families almost Plato, almost Shakespeare, or almost Goethe. Neither is it possible to trace the extraordinary powers of any of these back to any member of their ancestral line. Therefore, we can say that no other theory than that of Reincarnation can explain satisfactorily the causes which produce geniuses and prodigies in this world."[55]

Certainly, science and observation confirm the fact that heredity plays a part in certain physical manifestations of the child, as does environment. Color of eyes and hair, the stature and, sometimes, genetic diseases or deformities are a part of the contribution of parents and grandparents. Environment also plays a part, however, this influence occurs during development and might serve to alter or modify an attribute or characteristic, but it plays no part in the creation of those attributes or characteristics. In short, physical influences impact physical attributes while spiritual (non-physical) characteristics are the result of the spiritual seed that has developed over hundreds of years. These two components represent the plurality—physical and non-physical aspect of human existence.

The Parent/Child Relationship

It might be asked then, what about the parent/child relationship? Since the individual has already experienced many lives and parents, and since the character and personality have already been molded

---

[55] Abhedananda. (Kindle Locations 371-374)

throughout numerous lives, how does that impact the parent/child relationship?

There is no change in that relationship. The parents should remain the most powerful influence in a child's development. While the child will enter the world with the spiritual characteristics that it left with in the previous life, character building is still required in order for the child to move forward toward perfection. Understanding the concept of Reincarnation is valuable in helping parents understand where personality, talents and special abilities originate so they can nurture and encourage the further development of those personal assets.

"Consequently, environment has an undeniable influence, and it is perfectly true to say that the social conditions under which individuals are born favour or impede the development of their faculties. There its influence stops; it can intensify inequality, but does not create it."

Reincarnation and Inequality

The doctrine of Reincarnation offers the only reasonable solution to the inequalities that exist in our world. The truth is that there is no equality in physical life. From birth to death no one is equal. Tell the child that is born with an infirmity or a disability that they are equal to those who have been born without that disadvantage. Tell a child that has been raised in poverty that they are equal to those who have been raised in an affluent household. Tell those that have a lower IQ that they are equal to those with a higher IQ. While we may identify many similarities, equality will never exist. We are all different—unique.

Atkinson adds:

> "There are beings who, from the moment of their birth to the hour of their death, utter only cries of suffering and despair. What crime have they committed? Why are they here on earth? They have not petitioned to be here; and if they could, they would have begged that this fatal cup might be taken from their lips. They are here in spite of themselves, against their will. God would be unjust and wicked if he imposed so miserable an existence. But God is not unjust or wicked: the opposite qualities belong to his perfect essence.[56]

> "If, on the contrary, we admit the plurality of human existences and reincarnation—that is, the passage of the same soul through several

---

[56] William Walker Atkinson. (Kindle Locations 1037-1040).

bodies—all this is made wonderfully clear. Our presence on such or such a part of the earth is no longer the effect of a caprice of Fate, or the result of chance; it is merely a station in the long journey that we make through the world. Before our birth, we have already lived, and this life is the sequel and result of previous ones. We have a soul that we must purify, improve and ennoble during our stay upon earth; or having already completed an imperfect and wicked life, we are compelled to begin a new one, and thus strive to rise to the level of those who have passed on to higher planes."[57]

It has been said that what we are is determined by what we have been, and what we shall be is determined by what we are now. Equality cannot exist simply because no two lives have been lived the same. In one life an individual works to develop their talent and in the next they are attracted to that same field of endeavor, and they are able to excel because of their efforts in past lives. Architects, scholars, mathematicians, scientists, artists, philosophers, and the list goes on; there are those who excel over others. Why? Because these are the ones who have refined their skill, have accumulated knowledge and have acquired greater intelligence. They have made the best of past lives and they bear the fruits of those efforts in the present life.

Another factor when examining equality is evolution. Just as physical evolution occurs slowly, spiritual evolution also takes time. There are those who are at a very basic level of spiritual development. That condition might be for several reasons. It might be that

---

[57] Ibid., (Kindle Locations 1068-1073).

they have not lived many lives so they have not had the opportunity to participate in sufficient life cycles to have had the experiences necessary for spiritual growth. Therefore, they remain in a more animalistic, primitive state of existence. This is exemplified in those who are overly violent and seem to have no remorse for their actions. Their mind has not acquired the intelligence and other virtuous traits that are required for a more civilized existence.

On the other hand, an individual might have spent the majority of their lives in environments that did not provide growth opportunities. For instance, many third world countries stifle the accumulation of knowledge by lacking adequate avenues for knowledge gathering. Additionally, home environments where knowledge is not sought or taught limits progress. Whatever the cause, inequality exists from birth.

> "Souls, equal in potentialities whilst dormant as germs in the womb of Being, become unequal, as soon as they are born into existence in the manifested Universe, for they find predecessors, elder souls in front of them; inequality is intensified when they have reached the human stage,[58] where intelligence and will come into play, for henceforth, inequality in the actions of individuals, variations of what might be called merit and demerit, set up a second factor in the inequality of conditions. Evolution treasures up the causes that have not been able to germinate in one existence, and, by successive returns to earth, realises the aims and ends of that Justice

---

[58] The "human stage" here refers to the stage of consciousness or the stage of reasonable decision-making.

which governs the Universe, the designs of that Love which makes for progress and leads to perfection."[59]

---

[59] Ibid.

"Good and evil are like the up and down or the crest and hollow of a wave in the sea. A wave cannot rise without making a hollow somewhere in the sea. So in the infinite ocean of reality innumerable waves are constantly rising. The summit of each wave is called good, while the hollow beside it is evil or misery and the current of each individual life is constantly flowing towards the ultimate destination which we call perfection."

--Swami Abhedananda
Five Lectures on Reincarnation

Reincarnation and Justice

The doctrine of Reincarnation addresses the idea of justice more efficiently and fairly than any other religion or philosophy. In other ideologies God is delegated as the judge wielding the hammer of justice against the sinners of the world. Mixed with mercy for some and hell for others, God chooses who will be blessed and who will be cursed. The result for the Spirit of those being judged is either the blessing of heaven or paradise, or the curse of hell.

Contrarily, in Reincarnation, the concept of justice, referred to as Divine Justice, is grounded in the Law of Cause and Effect (action and consequence). Justice is a function of this world and it plays out in this world. Its effect impacts the spiritual as well as the physical.

It is here, through Divine Justice, that we find the only true example of equality. With Divine Justice all actions and deeds are evaluated fairly and without discrimination of any kind from life to life.

> "Nothing is ever lost; causes that have not fructified remain potential; and, like the grain of corn gathered thousands of years ago, grow and develop as soon as favourable soil and environment are offered them. Debts are still recorded, when the perishable sheaths of our physical bodies have been cast off; they come up for future payment, often in the next life. But this next life may not wipe off the whole of the liabilities, so the process is continued for several successive existences, ...Such is the truth."

The previous claim that "Nothing is ever lost;" covers a lot of issues. The first is the idea that upon physical death nothing of life is lost. In other words, our efforts, our deeds and our labors are not in vain. They weren't valuable only in this one short existence. Good deeds are payment forward. Contrarily, our bad deeds, those actions and words that caused hurt or injury to someone else become debts (consequence) that must be paid. Whether in the current life or subsequent lives, all debts must be paid. This is justice, but this justice is one that is consistently pushing in the direction of improvement and toward the good.

In the doctrine of Reincarnation, God does not punish for mistakes or for actions that hurt others. What we experience because of our actions is merely a result of cause and effect. For instance, if I touch a hot stove I will get burned. God didn't burn me because I touched the stove. I got burned because *I* touched a hot stove. *I* am responsible for touching the stove so I am responsible for getting burned. And, furthermore, I will get burned every time I touch the hot stove. If I didn't, I might think that the next time I touched the stove I wouldn't get burned and so, consequently, I would possibly never learn not to touch something that is hot. Cause and effect must be consistent if we are to learn and grow from our experiences. God is not responsible for our pain. We are.

There are no "rewards" and there is no "punishment" in Reincarnation. There is only action and consequence. In other words, good deeds result in positive consequences and bad deeds result in negative consequences because that's the natural law. But, as in our example above, the consequences, both positive and negative are always consistent. Negative consequences, then, are not a curse they are an opportunity to improve in the future by demonstrating how committing bad deeds result in pain and suffering, or other negative ramifications.

In the doctrine of Reincarnation everything happens for the good of the individual. There is a familiar analogy that uses a glass of water that is filled half way with water. The optimist says that the glass is half full, the pessimist declares that the glass is half empty.[60] The optimist sees the potential for more filling, but the pessimist only sees the water disappearing. When discussing the results of harmful behavior, when one sees the ramifications of such actions as punishment, they say the glass is half empty. It is a negative perspective of the situation. There is no hope, or very little hope for improvement. However, when the consequences are viewed as discipline, the glass is half full because as a result of learning from the experience, there is room for more water, or improvement; even though the consequences may be harsh and painful.

The consequences of harmful actions might be through any adverse situation or condition: hardship, sickness or many other forms of pain and suffering. However, these are not inflicted by anyone or anything. These consequences are the result of natural law. We must, once again, acknowledge that even in adversity there is opportunity for improvement. We should not be concerned about the cause of the hardship, which is temporary or even unknown, but, more importantly, how we will *respond or react* to the condition that has come into our life as a result of our actions. It is during

---

[60] This is anticipating that the ultimate goal is the filling of the glass with water and not emptying it.

these times more than any other that we grow in character, realizing how our actions impact our own life and the lives of others now and in the future. Pain and suffering is not the result of an angry God. It is the result of our own actions and decisions.

> "If we enjoy, we have earned it; if we suffer, we have earned it; in both cases through our own endeavors and efforts, and not by "chance," nor by reason of the merits or demerits of our forefathers, nor because of "predestination" nor "election" to that fate. If this be true, then one is given the understanding to stoically bear the pains and miseries of this life without cursing Fate or imputing injustice to the Divine. And likewise he is given an incentive toward making the best of his opportunities now, in order to pass on to higher and more satisfactory conditions in future lives."[61]

Christianity, Islam and Judaism are in conflict with the concept of Divine Justice. Christian theology teaches that everyone is born in sin (the sin of Adam, the first man). The doctrine asserts that in order to erase that sin a person needs to be "saved" so they will not be sent to Hell when they die. Hell is the punishment for the sins that that they have committed, or for the sin that Adam committed, and for which everyone is held accountable. Since no one can "save" themselves, a savior is required. Therefore, God came to earth in the form of a human named Jesus and he took upon himself the sins of all mankind and paid the price for every human's sins by being crucified on the cross. When an individual accepts this "Gospel" by professing that

---

[61] William Walker Atkinson.

Jesus was the Son of God who died for their sins, they are "saved" and their sins, all of their wrongdoings, are forgiven. All future sins are then forgiven by repenting, that is, expressing sincere sorrow and regret for committing those sins. Once adequately confessed, the confessor is once again free from guilt. Finally, when a person dies, their Soul goes either directly to heaven or to a place of waiting (depending on which denominational doctrine one believes) until they are resurrected at some point in the future, having been given new bodies, but ones that resemble the old ones that they had on earth (when Jesus was resurrected he was recognized by those who saw him. His body was similar to the one he had when he was alive on earth). Now, let me explain why this ideology discourages character development and defies the Law of Divine Justice.

First of all, this theology is contrary to the basic concept of justice which is necessary under the universal law of cause and effect (action and consequence). Universally, for every action there is a consequence, an effect that is the result of a cause. When a person is taught that someone else can assume the responsibility for their behavior then they no longer need to feel responsible for their actions or the consequences that result from those actions. Even though *they* were the cause, they are not held responsible for the effect. This invalidates the law of cause and effect. On the other hand, justice demands that the offender (the cause) be held responsible for their offense (the effect). This is also called fairness. When an individual is not held accountable for their own actions, or believes that they are not accountable, they lose sight of the reality of cause and effect; fairness is not achieved. Furthermore, the elimination of guilt prevents character building. Guilt exists for a reason. It is a reminder of the decisions that were made that had a negative affect on someone else. It is a reminder of the hurt that was caused and it is a warning not to repeat the same harmful behavior. Those who do not feel remorse or guilt for their hurtful actions are likely to repeat that behavior.

Islamic doctrine is very similar. Salvation comes through belief in Allah as the one God and in the Islamic doctrine. Forgiveness comes from repentance.

Additionally, these religions profess that in the span of a single lifetime a person can commit sins (wrongdoings) and for those sins be sentenced to everlasting damnation in a place of eternal punishment. If we look closely at such an idea, we can easily understand how unfair this concept is. The great philosopher, René Descartes observed that the finite cannot know or fully comprehend the infinite. Eternity is a length of time that is unknown to us. We have never experienced it and therefore we cannot grasp a time without end. Today an individual lives around 80 years or so, less than a nano-second in the aeons of time that have been. And yet, it is taught that an individual can make a decision in those few short years that will result in an eternity of punishment. This cannot be just because there is no crime that merits a punishment that lasts for eternity.

> "On the one hand, the orthodox theologians hold that for the deeds, good or evil, performed by a man during his short lifetime of a few years, and then performed under conditions arbitrarily imposed upon him at birth by his

Creator, man is rewarded or punished by an eternity of happiness or misery—heaven or hell. Perhaps the man has lived but one or two years of reasonable under-standing—or full three-score and ten—and has violated certain moral, ethical or even religious laws, perhaps only to the extent of refusing to believe something that his reason absolutely refused to accept—for this he is doomed to an everlasting sojourn in a place of pain, misery or punishment, or a state equivalent thereto. Or, on the other hand, he has done the things that he ought to have done, and left undone the things that he ought not to have done—even though this doing and not-doing was made very easy for him by reason of his environment and surroundings—and to crown his beautiful life he had accepted the orthodox creeds and beliefs of his fathers, as a matter of course—then this man is rewarded by an eternity of bliss, happiness and joy—without end. Try to think of what ETERNITY means—think of the æons upon æons of time, on and on, and on, forever—and the poor sinner is suffering exquisite torture all that time, and in all time to come, without limit, respite, without mercy! And all the same time, the "good" man is enjoying his blissful state, without limit, or end, or satiety! And the time of probation, during which the two worked out their future fate, was as a grain of sand as compared with the countless universes in space in all eternity—a relation which reduces the span of man's lifetime to almost absolutely NOTHING, mathematically considered. Think of this—is this Justice?

"And on the other hand, from the point of view of the Reincarnationist, is not the measure of cause and effect more equitably adjusted, even if we regard it as a matter of "reward and punishment"—a crude view by the way—when we see that every infraction of the law is followed by a corresponding effect, and an adherence to the law by a proportionate effect. Does not the "punishment fit the crime" better in this case—the rewards also. And looking at it from a reasonable point of view, devoid from theological bias, which plan seems to be the best exemplification of Justice and Natural Law, not to speak of the higher Divine Justice and Cosmic Law?"[62]

Here we should stress that what we are talking about are the spiritual rather than the physical consequences of behavior. The physical and social repercussions of our actions are still very much in effect.

I should emphasize that not all pain and suffering is the result of past-life behavior. Suffering is also the result of living in a world governed by the Law of Polarity (opposites). Suffering is the opposite value of happiness. One emotion is necessary for the existence of the other. Together, they provide a complete life experience that is essential for spiritual growth.

Pain and suffering are also the result of naturally occurring conditions such as genetic illnesses or

---

[62] Atkinson.

deformities. And then there is the greatest perpetrator of offenses: man.

> "But the most powerful causes of pain, due to multiplicity, are the ignorance and the will of beings who have reached the human stage. Man can employ his mental faculties for good or evil, and so long as he does not know definitely that he is the brother of all beings, i.e., until his divine faculties have been developed, and love and the spirit of sacrifice have taken possession of his heart, he remains a terrible egoist, more to be dreaded than the criminal dominated by a momentary burst of passion, for he acts in cold blood, he evades or refuses to recognise the law of humanity, he dominates and destroys."[63]

Diseases come and go; no one is immune. Injuries can be the result of someone else's actions; action and consequence is no respecter of age or gender. The cause of pain is secondary to how one responds to that condition. In the Old Testament there is the story of a man named Job who experiences excruciating pain from an illness. His friends assume that the illness is the result of sin in his life even though he knows that it is not. Rather than to lay blame for the illness, he uses the illness as an opportunity to cultivate patience, a virtue that will prove valuable in his present life and all subsequent lives.

I would like to add two important notes here. First, there is never an occasion where the innocent is used to discipline the guilty. In other words, a child born with a disease is not due to the sins of the parents. That would

---

[63] Théophile Pascal. (Kindle Locations 604-608).

not be just or fair to the innocent child. In Divine Justice, everyone is responsible for facing the consequences of their own actions.

Secondly, some of the ancients believed that a person who was excessively evil in one life might return as something other than human in the next. In other words, they might return in a subsequent life as an animal or bird or some other creature.

> "There is a good philosophy for Living and Dying. And, this being true, though you may have to "come back," you will not have to "go back," or fall behind in the Scale of Advancement or Spiritual Evolution—for it must always be Onward and Upward on the Ladder of Life! Such is the Law!"[64]

If we use physical evolution as a model for understanding spiritual evolution, we can easily observe how physical evolution always moves the species forward toward the ideal. It never works in reverse to diminish the object in any way. Likewise, an individual might not progress substantially from one life to the next due to a lack of character building, but the result would never be that the individual would return in a future life as something less than human once they have reached the elevated state of consciousness.

Who Judges?

Now comes an important question that must be addressed. When good deeds are done or bad deeds are committed, who assesses the deeds and determines the consequences for each? To answer that question, we

---

[64] Atkinson.

have to look again at the natural processes and laws of the world in which we live.

Let's assume that a rock is thrown into a pool of water. When the rock hits the water it becomes the cause of several effects. One consequence is that ripples form and move in a circular motion away from where the rock struck the water. If we know the size and weight of the rock and the velocity at which it hit the water; and we know the viscosity of the water, its depth and several other variables, we should be able to calculate the size of the ripples and the speed at which they will move away from the initial point of contact, and at what distance they will fade away. Now, no supernatural computer-operating angel had to sit there and calculate all of those determinants before the ripples could occur. The outcome has already been written into the operation of the world and the consequences have been predetermined based on those specific parameters. Reactions occur instantaneously. And, given the same identical parameters, the consequences of the rock hitting the water will be the same every time.

> "Everything is first worked out in the unseen before it is manifested in the seen, in the ideal before it is realized in the real, in the spiritual before it shows forth in the material. The realm of the unseen is the realm of cause. The realm of the seen is the realm of effect. The nature of effect is always determined and conditioned by the nature of its cause."[65]

You see, there are constants that have been designed into the operation of our universe.

---

[65] Ralph Waldo Trine. *In Tune with the Infinite; or, Fullness of Peace, Power, and Plenty*

"Throughout all of the formulations of the basic theories of physics and their application to the real world, there appear again and again certain fundamental invariant quantities. These quantities, called the fundamental physical constants, and which have specific and universally used symbols, are of such importance that they must be known to as high an accuracy as is possible. They include the velocity of light in vacuum (c); the charge of the electron, the absolute value of which is the fundamental unit of electric charge (e); the mass of the electron (m_e); Planck's constant (h); and the fine-structure constant."[66]

These constants make it possible for science to accurately investigate the mysteries of the universe. Without these unchanging factors there would be no physical science. The world would be in chaos. Given that these principles are consistent, no one needs to administer their behavior. They simply exist as part of the operation of our world—designed and incorporated into the universe from the very beginning. Likewise, when it comes to actions, every aspect of every doing has been meticulously established and is instantaneously applied to every action and reaction. That means that every good deed, no matter how seemingly insignificant, carries with it certain positive benefits. Every bad deed results in specific negative consequences. Every motive, attitude, and ramification is known in detail so that a positive or negative outcome is apportioned perfectly—justly and fairly. There is no need for an assessor or lengthy deliberation. The

---

[66] Physics/nist.gov. *Introduction to the constants for non-experts.*

process has been written into the functioning of the world from the beginning of time.

This is a fair and reasonable process—science and nature operating efficiently through the application of constants. Understanding these things, how can anyone doubt the presence or reality of an intelligent Being? Every scientific discovery reveals the work of an awesome and indescribably intelligent Creator.

Pain and Suffering in Children

The suffering, pain and death of children are viewed as more devastating than when those same things happen to adults. How can the consequences of a former life be administered fairly when it comes to the suffering of a child? The answer is, it can't. As mentioned previously, not all hardships are a result of behavioral consequences. Diseases and other natural maladies are no respecter of age. They strike as a natural occurrence to anyone at any age and at any time. But how do we know that suffering in children does not occur as a result of behavioral consequences? Again, as mentioned previously, all consequences are designed to advance the soul toward goodness, or improvement. Until a child reaches the age of consciousness, that is, the age of awareness, it does not have the capability to understand the lessons of action and consequence; nor does it have the capacity to find opportunities for improvement through hardships. And, if one reason for discipline is to lead one to goodness, it would not serve any purpose in children. Therefore, it would not be fair or just.

So, why must children suffer? Pragmatically speaking, it is because they are human. The laws of nature, the code of the universe is written for the good of the universe and all things therein. There are no caveats or exceptions. They apply to all objects and persons regardless of age or gender or species. Why is a helpless lion cub killed and devoured by jackals? Why do the young fall prey as food in practically every species? It is written in the code of the universe. Age is of no consideration. The wellbeing of the universe and everything in it—as a whole, must be considered.

I realize that this is no comfort to those who have had children that have suffered or died in infancy, but this is the way it is. It is truth.

So, how does the teaching of Reincarnation offer hope to those who must face the hardship of suffering children? The first reassurance is that as a child grows it will develop special skills or a unique understanding because of its condition. We see examples of this frequently. Stevie Wonder was a legendary musician who was blind from birth. Frida Kahlo, a victim of polio at age 6 became a renowned artist, and, of course, Helen Keller, both deaf and blind became famous worldwide for her many accomplishments.

But additionally, and most importantly, the doctrine of Reincarnation teaches that this life is not the only one. This is not the only opportunity that a child will have to experience life to it fullest. And for the parent who loses a child in death, there is comfort in knowing that the child is not gone forever; that it will have another chance at life. This might not sooth the pain of loss, but there is an opportunity for peace and even joy in realizing that this life, as short as it might have been, was not all that there is. There is more. For just as God is eternal, we too, share in that immortality.

"As in earthly life where day turns into night and work gives way to rest day after day, so it is that the Soul travels from life's labor to a time of rest and restoration and then again to physical life in a constant progression. There is no beginning or ending, only the continuous flow of conscious existence moving from one plane to another."

Reincarnation and Time

The most difficult aspect of Reincarnation is understanding the concept of time. In this life, on this planet, we are ruled by time. What time is it? When? Eternity, forever, minutes, hours, seasons, the past, the future, age. All of these terms involve a measure of time. What's difficult to grasp is that time as we know it only exists on this planet. Nowhere else in the universe, as far as we know, is time measured like it is here on earth. Probably nowhere else is there another planet the exact size of ours that rotates at the same speed around the same size sun. In so many ways our earth is a unique planet. Given that our understanding of time is distinctive and that it influences so much of our lives, it is virtually impossible to fathom what life would be without time. And yet, that is what we must attempt to do if we are to understand the concept of rebirth.

It might seem like events that occur in a world absent of linear time would be no more than random occurrences. But time is not the only method for quantifying order or chronology. What provides coherence to events when there is no measure of time is their relationship one with the other. One thing occurs and then another occurs in an orderly sequence. Without time, and because life never dies, birth and death are no more than events that occur as part of the sequence of cause and effect, but they do not signify the beginning or end of anything.

Throughout history, a circle symbolized eternity. That's because a circle doesn't seem to have a beginning or end.

However, it is sometimes difficult to visualize a circle as a continuum. For me, personally, I prefer an endless line, but one that is slanted slightly upward, signifying the slow, but steady evolution of the Soul.

As in earthly life where day turns into night and work gives way to rest day after day, so it is that the Soul travels from life's labor to a time of rest and restoration and then again to physical life in a constant progression. There is no beginning or ending, only the continuous flow of conscious existence moving from one plane to another. And, as the Soul progresses along its inevitable journey, it evolves toward perfection, or digresses due to its desire for materialism—fame and fortune.

Understanding the concept of time, or its absence, allows us to realize how throughout human history we witness amazing events that seem to be without explanation. How did the ancient Egyptians learn to build elaborate pyramids centuries before that knowledge was available? How did the Romans construct their elaborate aquifers? These things become clear if we understand that the period between lives is timeless. There is no past, present or future. Therefore, an individual might be born into the physical world at any point in human history since there is no requirement for a rebirth to be limited to linear time or sequential progression.

These amazing events and many more like them were the products of men and women who had lived in a "future" time but were reborn in a "past" time. How was Plato and Socrates able to expound so profoundly on subjects unfamiliar to most? Were these men years ahead of their time, or were they living in years past their time?

The question may be asked, will Souls know or make contact with earthly relations during the afterlife? Once again, whatever we say about the afterlife, or that time between lives, is purely speculation. However, if it is true that nothing is lost from life to life and memories are still fresh during the afterlife for the purpose of review, then it seems logical to assume that we should recognize, in some form or fashion, those with whom we have had earthly ties. We cannot speculate as to the duration between physical lives, but if we are allowed to review our earthly experiences it would be reasonable to presume that it would require a significant length of time. So, parents or maybe even relatives of former generations might be available for intercourse. Plato suggested that there would be a thousand years between earthly lives. Others suggest that those who die at a younger age will have less to learn from their experiences so they will return to a new life sooner than those who experienced a longer life on earth. Psychiatrist Jim Tucker, the expert in past life memories in children quoted earlier, says that his studies indicate that an individual might return as a new life in as little as 16 months.

However, what form our Soul will take in the afterlife is unknown. One thing is certain, we will not have a physical form because we will be in a non-physical dimension. We are, in reality, not physical creatures. We are spiritual beings just as God is. How can we interact in a world where there is no physical appearance or material forms? It's impossible to say.

But just as we are social creatures on the physical plane, it is safe to surmise that we will also be socially active in the dimension beyond.

"Until we find out who was born this time around, it seems irrelevant to seek earlier identities. I have heard many people speak of who they believe they were in previous incarnations, but they seem to have very little idea of who they are in this one. . ... Let's take one life at a time. Perhaps the best way to do that is to live as though there were no afterlife or reincarnation. To live as though this moment was all that was allotted."

— Stephen Levine
A Year to Live: How to Live This
Year as If It Were Your Last

Reincarnation and Perfection

As we have discussed, life on earth is dualistic. In other words, as long as we are on the earth we are constructed of two conflicting natures: physical and non-physical (spiritual). As we journey from life to life, we should evolve to be more spiritual and less physical. We should become less concerned with material or tangible things—that is, if we have improved from one life to the next. If not, we might not develop our spiritual nature as much as we could have and, therefore, retain a predominately materialistic nature, slowing down our progress to perfection and requiring us to remain locked in the cycle of rebirth for a longer period of time. This is explained in the Vedanta:

> "Again as the purpose and method of natural laws are uniform throughout the universe, the end of intellectual, moral and spiritual evolution will be attained when intellectual, moral and spiritual perfection are acquired. Intellectual perfection means perfection of intellect; and intellect is perfect when we understand the true nature of things and never mistake the unreal for the real, matter for spirit, non-eternal for eternal, or vice versa. Moral perfection consists in the destruction of selfishness; and spiritual perfection is the manifestation of the true nature of spirit which is immortal, free, divine and one with the Universal Spirit or God."[67]

Reincarnation teaches that a Soul must participate in the cycle of life and death over and over until it has

---

[67] Swami Abhedananda. *Five Lectures on Reincarnation.*

achieved perfection. But what does that mean? How can we become perfect? Realizing that we do exist in a physical world that has tremendous influence over us how can we escape from material things and become totally spiritual? Are we to become reclusive, separating ourselves from the rest of society? Are we to live as beggars without a home or work? Are we to neglect our own health and the physical things that are required for survival like food, clothing and shelter? Sexual desire is a natural instinct for sustaining the human species. Are we to become celibate and ignore one of the strongest urges inherent in humans? The answer is yes and no.

Sages of old and many of the great teachers of antiquity, as well as many religious leaders of today, advocate the total abandonment of material possessions and desires. Likewise. the Upanishads (Vedanta) seem to teach the total abandonment of duality.

A side note here: In reading this quote it is important to remember that every religion has its own name for God. The Hindus call the ultimate Supreme Being, Brahman. Westerners can substitute the name God for Brahman. In truth, the Creator is beyond all names.

> "Brahman cannot be realized by those
> Who are subject to greed, fear, and anger.
> Brahman cannot be realized by those
> Who are subject to pride of name and fame
> Or the vanity of scholarship.
> Brahman cannot be realized by those
> Who are enmeshed in life's duality.
> But to all those who pierce this duality,
> Whose hearts are given to the Lord of Love,
> He gives Himself through his infinite grace,
> He gives Himself through his infinite grace."[68]

According to his biography, Siddhartha Gautama, the Buddha, born into wealth, gave up all material possession and traveled the world in search of enlightenment. At one time, it is said, that he was eating as little as one grain of rice a day. It was then that he realized that self-denial wasn't accomplishing anything—not for himself or anyone else. He later taught that the middle road was the one to travel: moderation. His teaching advocated character improvement through introspection.

So how can we understand these teachings and how do we live in a physical world without having some touch with the material things that we need to survive? The answer has been taught over and over and it has been overlooked and misinterpreted for thousands of years. In the Brihadaranyaka Upanishad, it is written:

> "As a person acts, so he becomes in life. Those who do good become good; those who do harm become bad. Good deeds make one pure; bad deeds make one impure. You are what your deep, driving desire is. As your desire is, so is your will. As your will is, so is your deed. As your deed is, so is your destiny."[69]

It's true that we need certain material things in a material world. In order to get these things we must work for them. And to be successful in keeping our job we must be diligent in doing what the job requires. We must be responsible for our families and we must be involved in caring for our world. These are among the

---

[68] *The Tejobindu Upanishad.* Vs. 6. Translated by Eknath Easwaran. (Nilgiri Press).
[69] *The Brihadaranyaka Upanishad.* Verse 5b. Translated by Eknath Easwaran, (Nilgiri Press, Canada, 2007)

things that we must do as responsible human beings existing in a physical, materialistic world. The question is, where is our *desire*? Or, said another way: where is our heart? The key is desire. As the writer so wisely put it, "You are what your deep, driving desire is". We can possess the material things that we need but we should possess them out of need. If our need becomes our burning desire then we have become materialistic and we no longer grow spiritually. If we desire a bigger home when the one we have is sufficient, or a big boat or any other non-necessity, then our desire is misplaced and we are tilting the scale in the direction of materialism. If, on the other hand, we desire to be a better person and that is where our focus is, our sincerest intent, then we are becoming less materialistic and moving closer to spirituality. Our desire—what we want, drives our actions, and our actions define who we are. "As your deed (action) is, so is your destiny."

The following quotation from a writer on the subject, gives clearly and briefly the Reincarnationist argument regarding this point. The writer says:

> "Desire for other forms of earthly experience can only be extinguished by undergoing them. It is obvious that any one of us, if now translated to the unseen world, would feel regret that he had not tasted existence in some other situation or surroundings. He would wish to have known what it was to possess wealth and rank, or beauty, or to live in a different race or climate, or to see more of the world and society. No spiritual ascent could progress while earthly longings were dragging back the soul, and so it frees itself from them by successively securing them and dropping them. When the round of

such knowledge has been traversed, regret for ignorance has died out."[70]

In other words, as we experience life and obtain those tangible things that we think will make life better, but then, after obtaining them, realize how unfulfilling they are, we are led to understand the worthlessness of worldly things and the value of non-physical (spiritual) things. Some people need to experience more than others in order to grasp this truth. However, when we do understand this truth, giving up worldly things will come naturally. Our desire will be for the intangible—caring for others and, by doing so, caring for ourselves and building a strong and virtuous character that will move us, life by life, closer to perfection.

You see, it's a matter of perspective—how we view our objective. Some people will strive to give up material things and find themselves overwhelmed and unsuccessful because they are concentrating on the very things that they are trying to overcome. However, if we take the approach that we are attempting to be more virtuous and we focus on achieving something rather than on giving something up, our energy is moving in a positive direction rather than a negative one. We are *gaining* something rather than giving something up. There is no sacrifice in Reincarnation. The word sacrifice means *the act of giving up something valued for the sake of something else regarded as more important or worthy*. When an individual realizes the value of spiritual attainment then material things become less important. Our desire is redirected. When this level of spiritual maturity is reached, material things are just not considered valuable.

---

[70] William Walker Atkinson.

The Wealthy and Perfection

Does that mean that a wealthy person cannot reach perfection? Remember, Jesus is quoted as saying,

> "Again I tell you, it is easier for a camel to go through the eye of a needle than for someone who is rich to enter the kingdom of God."[71]

You see, if we look again at cause and effect, there are certain rewards for doing things well. The result of building a successful business is, perhaps, the accumulation of wealth. However, if wealth is the result and not the objective of the business; if the individual's desire is to build a business (because that's what he was led to do by his intuition) and not for the accumulation of wealth, then wealth is not a negative asset. In fact, if that wealth is used in a positive way to help others, then wealth actually contributes to character building. Jesus offers this caution to the wealthy because when one has an abundance of wealth, it's a great temptation to use that wealth to indulge in worldly or physical consumption.

Finding Peace in Life

As we focus on the "good" things and develop within ourselves the "will" to do what is good, then with each earthly life we will move further and further away from the duality of earthly existence. There are those who eventually reach the place where their total desire is for spiritual fulfillment. Jesus, Saint Teresa and many of the sages of old successfully reached this place of perfection. I'm sure there are many others who have achieved this station who did not have the notoriety of

---

[71] Matthew 19:24

those named. But, can *we* really achieve perfection? Jesus thought we could. He is credited with saying:

> "Be perfect, therefore, as your heavenly Father is perfect."[72]

As we have discussed, every Soul is unique. There are no two Souls alike in personality, talent, interests, ability or character. So it is that the road to perfection is different for every person. Each of us meticulously constructs our own destiny, chooses our own path, makes our own way.[73] That's the reason why we are all exactly where we should be at this time in our journey. We should not compare ourselves to others, thinking that we are better or worse off. Each of us is exactly where we are meant to be because, from decision to decision, from action to reaction, we have dictated our own destiny.

> "But, after all, if there is Ultimate Justice in the plan, working ever and ever for our good and advancements, as the Reincarnationists claim—then it must follow that each of us is in just the best place for his own good at the present moment, and will always be in a like advantageous position and condition."[74]

It might not be where we want to be, but it is where we should be and where we need to be. When we realize that we are where we are because of our own decisions, we begin to understand how important every decision is. We also learn to recognize how important it is to view every situation as an opportunity to grow spiritually, refraining from anger, or envy or impatience

---

[72] Matthew 5:48
[73] Predestination and free will are discussed later.
[74] William Walker Atkinson.

or stress, but rather using each experience to improve who we are in this life and the next.

Certainly, there are those who will become impatient in their efforts to attain perfection. When we set goals that are too high there is the danger of becoming disenchanted or depressed at our lack of significant progress toward that goal. We might even decide to simply give up. But, just as physical evolution occurs slowly, so it is with spiritual evolution. The journey is slow. It occurs each and every day with each and every decision. And when we fall short— when we make the wrong decision and feel like we have not met our own expectations, we must realize that we are exactly where we are supposed to be at this stage of our evolution. We must do what we are able to do and feel satisfied and contented with what we have accomplished. Success will come slowly but steadily, day after day.

Reincarnation and Predestination

In this dissertation I have often said that Reincarnation teaches that every individual is responsible for their own destiny; that each life builds on previous lives. But how does that fit with the concept of predestination? Hasn't the Creator predestined the universe to exist as it does? Didn't God, through evolution, predetermine the shape and form of all things? If we believe that the universe had a Creator and that the Creator had a design for all things as we have shown in this discussion, then the answer is, once again, "yes and no". Allow me to explain.

To understand my explanation, it is necessary to acknowledge the following assumptions:

- That it is more reasonable to believe that there is a supernatural entity that created the world than to believe that one does not exist (see earlier discussion);
- That this entity is omnipresent in that it has always existed and will always exist and that it is not limited by time or space since it is beyond all universal laws that impact our lives. In other words, there is no linear time—no past and no future. Everything is in the present. This fact helps us to understand God's omniscience. God has been there, seen that and has the t-shirt. There are those who claim that God's knowledge is limited to the past and present. But that nullifies God's omniscience. Under that concept, God's knowledge is imperfect.

So, how does all of this impact predestination? Certainly, it's true to assume that if God created the universe, God did so with a plan and purpose. And, judging from the evolution of our universe, it is, and has been, functioning perfectly in accordance with that plan. That is, if it has operated efficiently in the past, there is no reason to believe it will not do so in the future. There are those who will look for flaws in nature and claim that these apparent faults are proof that the universe is not perfect. However, that is an inaccurate assumption simply because we cannot know what God's plan for the universe is. Therefore, we are in no position to determine whether or not the universe is operating as intended. Surely, the dinosaurs would say that their extinction was a flaw in the design of the world since it didn't turn out very well for them. However, today, we would certainly be inclined to condone their extinction by pointing out that climate change is a fact of nature, and that their survival could possibly have led to our extinction! Perspective plays an influential role in our evaluation of how we view the evolving world. So, since all things seem to have a purpose in existing, we must assume that the universe also has a purpose and a destiny. That destiny we would say has been preordained. But how about humans? Is our life and destiny predestined?

The purpose of physical evolution is the goal of attaining perfection—that is, bringing every creature and organism to its fullest potential. Likewise, spiritual evolution has the same goal—the perfection of the Soul. So, the preordained destiny of every human is spiritual perfection. That preordained fate will eventually be achieved by everyone. However, the journey to that destination, the path that we take, depends totally on *our* decisions. Therefore, we, and we alone, are responsible for every step of our pilgrimage. Our decisions are our own. They are not made for us. Let me offer an example. Let's suppose that I have a son who loves chocolate. I know him well and I know how much he craves candy. So, when I offer him an apple or a chocolate bar I already know which one he will take. And, just as I anticipated, he takes the chocolate. However, my foreknowledge of him and his desire for candy had no bearing on his decision. The choice was his.

Let me offer another explanation. Once again, we must acknowledge that God is omnipresent. So, as we have discussed, there is no past or future with God in that God is everywhere at any time since there is no linear time that we know of outside of our own planet. We might make a decision today, but God already knows what that decision was because God sees tomorrow and, therefore, knows what decisions we have made today. So, God knows what our decisions will be but God didn't make them for us.

Does God participate in our decision-making? Of course. God is present through our intuition. God also assists us through a myriad of other sources like friends and family and knowledge that is available through books and even the internet. But, it is up to us to make the final decision.

As I have said, our predestined destiny is for perfection, however, how we make the trip is entirely up to us.

The secret to traveling a smooth road, then, is to use intuition (advice from past lives), commonsense, reason and knowledge when making decisions. For those who are wise the pilgrimage will be a brief and orderly journey. For others, however, the journey will be long and arduous requiring hundreds or even thousands of lifetimes—each lifetime having its own unique destiny.

"Do not believe in anything simply because you have heard it. Do not believe in anything simply because it is spoken and rumored by many. Do not believe in anything simply because it is found written in your religious books. Do not believe in anything merely on the authority of your teachers and elders. Do not believe in traditions because they have been handed down for many generations. But after observation and analysis, when you find that anything agrees with reason and is conducive to the good and benefit of one and all, then accept it and live up to it."

— Gautama Siddhartha
The Buddha

Reincarnation: The Conclusion

In this life I have sought knowledge and truth as objectively as possible. At times this search has brought me great despair when it revealed that what I had always been taught and believed was not credible. It has brought me confusion when it introduced concepts and doctrines that advocated ideas that did not make sense or were fabricated delusions of dreamers and mystics. But in the end, it has brought me peace and understanding for there is no authentic peace outside of truth. Where did I come from? Why am I the way I am? Why am I here? What really matters in life? What comes next? The study of life and death is the most significant study of all, and it was not until I discovered the ancient philosophy of Reincarnation that I finally realized the truth. Why do I believe it is the truth? Because it is supported by the Laws of the Universe; because it is a philosophy that makes life better and raises humans to a higher standard of existence; because it is reasonable and it makes sense.

It is the most essential philosophy to be learned and taught. Thousands of years ago it was only revealed to those who were "ready" to listen to its wisdom. They were the hand-picked intelligent and eager minds of the time. Today, it is a philosophy that is shared openly with the masses. However, there are still only a few who will listen and understand.

Thousands of years ago the sages of old said it this way:

> "As the Katha Upanishad says, only a few even hear these truths; of those who hear, only a few

understand and of those only a handful attain the goal."[75]

Reincarnation inspires us to try harder, to be the best we can be; to grow intellectually; to refine our skills; to develop our talents; and to be more God-like—showing compassion, demonstrating patience and sharing love.

Reincarnation teaches that we and only we are responsible for our future and our destiny. When it comes to our decisions there is no predestination. God isn't responsible for our calamity or our success. We are. God isn't responsible for what kind of person we are or what we will become. We are. We spend a lifetime preparing for the next. We work to build a virtuous character in this life so we can benefit from it in the next.

In Reincarnation there is no fear of death, only an expectation of good things to come. There is no fear of eternal punishment, only the assurance that all things work to improve the condition of the Soul. Realizing that we are all a part of the One life of the universe—that God is in all provides us with a sense of worth and an intimate connection with all things; God is in us and we are in God. There is an overwhelming urge to rejoice, acknowledging that everyone will someday reach perfection, and that pain and suffering are a necessary but short-lived part of the experience of life that leads to a virtuous character and happiness.

Reincarnation doesn't require participation in rituals or ceremonies. It doesn't call for obedience to any theology or religious ideology. There are no Reincarnation evangelical propagandists. In fact, it is

---

[75] *The Unpanishads*. Translated by Eknath Easwaran. (Nilgiri Press). 24

not even necessary that a person believe in Reincarnation. The truth is the truth. It doesn't matter if a person believes in gravity or not. It still exists and we are all subject to its law. Likewise, we are all moving in the same direction with the same goal. As a person moves from life to life, whether they believe in Reincarnation or not, as they strive to become a better person, they are moving toward the goal of perfection. And that is the doctrine of Reincarnation.

> "The great central fact in human life, in your life and in mine, is the coming into a conscious, vital realization of our oneness with this Infinite Life, and the opening of ourselves fully to this divine inflow. This is the great central fact in human life, for in this all else is included, all else follows in its train. In just the degree that we come into a conscious realization of our oneness with the Infinite Life, and open ourselves to this divine inflow, do we actualize in ourselves the qualities and powers of the Infinite Life."[76]

It has been my objective in this discourse to provide the reader with information concerning this most credible and reasonable philosophy regarding life and death. However, I fully understand that it is not for everyone. Reincarnation teaches that there is only one journey, but many paths that lead to the final destination. Every individual must find their own way—their own path. There might be those who read this who are completely satisfied and at peace with a particular religion or ideology to which they have committed their life. And that is well and good. If that religion does not result in

---

[76] Trine. In Tune with the Infinite; or, Fullness of Peace, Power, and Plenty

the harm or oppression of others and if it inspires spiritual growth then it is well and good to continue in that belief. A person's character is not determined by what they believe. It is determined by what they do. The final test is the way in which it works as a whole. "By their fruits you shall know them".

We must all ask what we are taking into the next life? What can we fix now so we don't need to fix it later? What talents and skills can we improve so they will be more useful in the next life? Where is our desire? Because where our desire is, there is our destiny.

> "And whatever may be the details of the Truth, the fact remains that whatever state awaits the soul finally, it must be Good, and in accordance with Divine Wisdom and Ultimate Justice and Universal Love.
>
> But whether this be true, or whether there is a place of final rest in the highest spiritual realms other than in the sense of absorption in the Divine, or whether there is a state of Eternal Progression from plane to plane, from realm to realm, on and on forever Godward, and more and more God-like—the End must be Good, and there is nothing to Fear, for "the Power that rules Here, rules There, and Everywhere. And remember this, ye seekers after ultimate truths—the highest authorities inform us that even the few stages or planes just ahead of us in the journey are so far beyond our present powers of conception, that they are practically unknowable to us—this being so, it will be seen that states very much nearer to us than the End must be utterly beyond the powers not only of our

understanding but also of our imagination, even when strained to its utmost. This being so, why should we attempt to speculate about The End? Instead, why not say... 'I do not ask to see the distant scene. One step enough for me—Lead Thou me on!'"[77]

---

[77] William Walker Atkinson.

Resource Material

Théophile Pascal. *Reincarnation: A Study in Human Evolution, The Resurrection of the Body and The Reincarnation of the Soul.* The Theosophical Publishing Society

William Walker Atkinson. *Reincarnation and the Law of Karma / A Study of the Old-New World-Doctrine of Rebirth, and Spiritual Cause and Effect.* Yogi Publication Society.

Swami Abhedananda. *Five Lectures on Reincarnation.* The Project Gutenberg. Urbana, Illinois.

Swami Paramananda. *The Upanishads.* The Project Gutenberg. Urbana, Illinois:

Plato. Phaedo; *The Last Hours Of Socrates.* Translator: Benjamin Jowett. The Project Gutenberg Urbana, Illinois.

Thomas Paine. *The Writings of Thomas Paine, Volume IV. (The Age of Reason Part l & ll).* 1794-1796. Editor: Moncure Daniel Conway. The Project Gutenberg. Urbana, Illinois.

Ralph Waldo Trine. *In Tune with the Infinite; or, Fullness of Peace, Power, and Plenty.* London George Bell & Sons.

William James. *The Varieties of Religious Experience: A Study in Human Nature.* The Gifford Lectures on Natural Religion Delivered in Edinburgh in 1901-1902. Longmans, Green, and Co. New York

David Presti & Dr. Bruce Greyson. *Mind Beyond Brain: Buddhism, Science and the Paranormal.* Columbia University Press - 2018

Made in the USA
Coppell, TX
20 January 2026

67277830R00111